Shameless

Shameless

An 8-Week Study to Freedom
Through God's Redemption

DEBBIE VANDERSLICE

NEW HOPE
PUBLISHERS

Birmingham, Alabama

New Hope® Publishers
P. O. Box 12065
Birmingham, AL 35202-2065
www.newhopepublishers.com

New Hope Publishers is a division of WMU®.

Library of Congress Cataloging-in-Publication Data

Vanderslice, Debbie, 1967-
  Shameless : an 8-week study to freedom through God's redemption /
Debbie Vanderslice.
     p. cm.
  ISBN 978-1-59669-216-9 (sc)
  1. Christian women--Religious life--Textbooks. 2. Shame in the
Bible--Textbooks. 3. Shame--Religious
aspects--Christianity--Textbooks.. I. Title.
  BV4527.V37 2008
  248.8'43071--dc22
                         2008030625

Cover designer: Birdsong Creative www.birdsongcreative.com
Interior page designer: Sherry Hunt

ISBN-10: 1-59669-216-2
ISBN-13: 978-1-59669-216-9

N084139 • 1008 • 3.5M1

Dedication

To my daughter, Hannah

What a beautiful, caring, and amazing young lady you have become. Nothing brings me greater joy than to see you growing strong in the Lord. I am so proud of you and your generous heart. Keep on keeping on. I love you.

To Sherry

I could never thank you enough for your support and encouragement over the years. You have taught me so much in life. All I can do is live one day at a time and remember the things you have said to me. You are one of the greatest gifts in my life.

To Joy

I am overwhelmed at your giving spirit. Thank you for opening your heart to me and giving me hope for the future.

Contents

The Revolving Door of Shame
Eve

Since Creation, God has allowed humans to make choices and experience consequences. Adam and Eve's decision to disregard and disobey God's commands led to their fall and the deadly shame that Satan brought—to them and to us. But there is *good* shame, too, that comes from God, convicting us of our sins. Though Satan tells us we are worthless, filthy, and defected, God convicts us with His exceedingly great love—along with His correction. We choose to receive His grace in the person of Jesus Christ. Our redemption is His glory.

Standing Tall with Broken Promises
Tamar

Tamar, a woman listed in Jesus's genealogy, dealt with the shame associated with others' broken promises to her—others who knew better. Tamar's father-in-law, Judah, deceived her through his complicity in breaking God's marriage laws. This deception resulted in Tamar continuing to endure the shame of barrenness, a distinctively difficult form of suffering for a woman. Although there was added deception, sin, and more shameful behavior on Tamar's part—to become pregnant by Judah—God remained faithful to all His laws and promises. The outcome of Tamar's shame was her redemption, to God's glory.

Any woman who has felt shame probably longs to see a pauper, such as Ruth, turned into a princess. Another woman in Jesus's genealogy, Ruth followed her heart and her widowed mother-in-law and went to a country, people, and God Ruth did not know. In her new lifestyle, Ruth humbly and obediently serves in her kinsman Boaz's fields and in her mother-in-law's home. What happens eradicates Ruth's reasons to feel shamed. In fact, God redeemed her life and exalted her. God's redemptive power has not changed and this relates to our lives as well.

Adultery. Pregnancy out-of-wedlock. Murder. Marriage to the murderer, a king. Death of an infant child. Birth of another son. Although mistakes plague everyone, not everyone's sins are visible for all to see…as were Bathsheba's errors with the man in charge of a nation. What can we do if the devil imprisons us with conscious guilt and shame over something we did or something that happened long ago?

Many say Rahab was a whore. Yet God used her to protect His people and to declare her faith in Him to her household and to history. God delights in taking sinful, impulse-ridden, and weak people to transform them into new creations. God also delights in using the unlikely person to declare His glory. Mary, mother of Jesus—impregnated by God. Can you imagine what would happen in today's world if an almost 15-year-old girl of lower income were to tell authorities the father of her baby were God? Mary faced enormous shame while carrying the King of kings.

PART 3

Scorning the Shame Forever
The Samaritan Woman and A Sinful Woman
The woman at the well and a sinful woman at Jesus's feet. Female outcasts. The defeated Samaritan woman at the well battled shame daily, ashamed of being herself. Is it any wonder Christ offered this woman Himself as living water? And what better example to see shame's response to God's love than the woman who washed Jesus's feet with her tears and her perfume treasure? God can transform a life of shame for His glory. The Cross equalizes everyone.

On the Fringe of Wholeness
Mary Magdalene and the Woman Who Bled
The woman who bled for 12 years; isn't it unfathomable? God takes a shamed woman and chooses her and her condition—bleeding—and accepts her when no one else would. Christ is familiar with suffering; it is a reality He knows so well. It is comforting to realize God knows exactly how we feel. Christ knows our shame and all the other feelings of suffering we have experienced.

Scorning the Shame
Us
Whether the hindrance is short-lived or calls for longsuffering, shame is at the root of the discouragement that comes against us. God's Word encourages us to consider Jesus and to throw off the hindrances of sin and shame we all face, and to experience His purposes for our lives. Jesus scorns shame and empowers us to do the same in our lives

Acknowledgments

This Bible study would not be possible without so many people.

To Joyce Dinkins, my editor, who was so patient, diligent, and encouraging. Thank you beyond words.

To Leigh Anne Bennett and Dolores, thank you for your support and care, especially during my time of need.

My deepest thanks to my friends at Fellowship Bible Church, Agape, and Celebrate Recovery.

Kristin Agar, thank you for all your support and encouragement.

And to the readers of this study, thank you for being so honest and real about your shame. Just like the women in this study, God can use our shame and turn it into His amazing glory.

Introduction

You've seen it countless times before, although you may not have recognized it as such. It has many faces yet tries to masquerade as invisible. Perhaps you saw shame today and didn't even know it—that thin lady down the street who runs morning, noon, and night yet still complains of "looking fat." Maybe you've seen the woman at church who seems to leap three ongoing Bible studies in a single bound and serves others nonstop—while her family consistently gets the leftovers of her time. Shame also may try to dress itself up as the beauty queen who outwardly appears one way while feeling like the most unattractive creature on the face of the earth. What about the career woman who seems to have it all together whenever you see her at home, church, or on the job, and yet she cannot seem to get rid of the bags under her eyes that tell the tale that sleep is an elusive peace in her not-so-perfect world?

Although shame is everywhere, we frequently don't know its true identity. We've seen shame's ugly face as it darts about and hides behind masks, such as *anorexia nervosa, bulimia, workaholism, substance abuse, depression, suicide, illicit sexual activity, abortion, and even false teaching and religiosity*. The list can—and does—go on. Perhaps *you* know shame intimately; you saw shame in the mirror today.

I don't know about you, but I sometimes run and hide from God. Why? Because I am for some reason ashamed, and afraid to give Him my shame. *I* try to fix my life. God wants us instead to run to Him, regardless of what has happened. We can either receive Satan's shame, or grasp onto Jesus for the things we have done that are not according to His plan, or even that which is shameful that has happened to us at the hands of another person.

In this study, we'll see clearly that God wants us do the latter. In Part 1, we see how God's Word reveals the source of this disease of shame, how Scripture points to the only

One who can heal us, and unlocks His eternal promises not to leave or forsake anyone of us to shame's curses. In fact, God does not relinquish anyone to a life of shame because of the redemption He has provided. Our loving heavenly Father urges each of us *"Come to me, all you who are weary and burdened and I will give you rest"* (Matthew 11:28). He does not want us to bear the burdens of shame and perish in life, but desires us to have abundant and everlasting life (John 10:10).

In Part 2, we'll review how God dealt blows to shame in the lives of five women in Jesus's lineage, redeeming them. In Part 3, our study encompasses the lives of other women Jesus touched with His healing redemption and how He can, likewise, redeem us.

Some chapter days have more questions than others; some of the questions require more self-examination. Though, the chapters with fewer questions still provide you with adequate opportunities to ponder how God's Word addresses our shame and how He wants us to respond to His love.

I invite you to explore afresh God's very real deliverance in the lives of many, including several women who are named in Christ's lineage and others whom God redeemed as a testimony to us. It is my prayer that this *Shameless* study will help to remind us that we have been set free, as we go to God with our shame—whatever the manifestation—to release it to the God who hung on the Cross, disregarding the shame.

PART 1

Shameless

The Revolving Door of Shame
Eve

When the woman saw that the fruit of the tree was good for food and pleasing to the eye, and also desirable for gaining wisdom, she took some to her husband, who was with her, and he ate it. Then the eyes of both of them were opened, and they realized they were naked; so they sewed fig leaves together and made coverings for themselves.
—Genesis 3:6–7

This week's focus is an examination of what *shame* is and how it destroys, by identifying its roots. Daily studies affirm that God alone is the Source for uprooting shame so that we can experience healing.

GOOD SHAME, BAD SHAME

God clearly instructed Adam with regard to his options in the Garden of Eden, warning him of the consequences of disobedience. Adam and Eve, in perfect union with God, traded the truth of this perfect fellowship with God, and instead chose Satan's deadly deception.

"You will not surely die," the serpent said to the woman. "For God knows that when you eat of it your eyes will be opened, and you will be like God, knowing good and evil."
—Genesis 3:4–5

Anytime there is *bad* shame, you can be sure that Satan is close by, quickly telling us we are defective in some way, that we are filthy and worthless.

It happened in the blink of an eye to Eve. In the snap of the fingers. In the beat of her heart. It happened so quickly she wasn't sure what to think or say. Or do. Silently, the lie had crawled up to her and before reality had time to sink in, she had slept in its bed. A dream she thought it would be. Rather, a charmed slumber turned into her worst nightmare. She had been promised the keys to the world, but awoke with merely the chains to hell.

If only she had listened. Listening could not have been that hard to do, yet she did not. So simple and yet so difficult for her. She had, so to speak, "let into her bed" the one partner God had said to keep away. That promise beside her turned out to be a lie from the chief of all liars. She had gone to sleep a queen in the garden of perfection and awakened as a captive in the prison of all cells. The charmer turned out to be a snake. The promise a lie. The keys of freedom that had once held the world at her beck and call, now tainted, held her captive to her own personal prison. Silently it happened. All was stolen. Eve was the partaker of the forbidden fruit and the revolving door of shame opened.

Week 1 • Day 1
The Reality of Shame

Now the serpent was more crafty than any of the wild animals the Lord God had made. He said to the woman, "Did God really say, 'You must not eat from any tree in the garden?'" The woman said to the serpent, "We may eat fruit from the trees in the garden, but God did say 'You must not eat fruit from the tree that is in the middle of the garden, and you must not touch it, or you will die.'" "You will not surely die," the serpent said to the woman. "For God knows that when you eat of it you will be like God, knowing good and evil. When the woman saw that the fruit of the tree was good for food and pleasing to the eye, and also desirable for gaining wisdom, she took some to her husband, who was with her, and he ate it. Then the eyes of both of them were opened, and they realized they were naked; so they sewed fig leaves together and made coverings for themselves.
—Genesis 3:1–7

God created a perfect world in which Eve and Adam lived. They walked and talked with God Almighty. They could eat from any tree in the Garden except one. Yet Eve bought Satan's lie and doubted God; she thought she was missing out on something. Maybe she felt God was holding back on her enjoyment or significance, though God had given her a perfect identity.

Read Genesis 3:2. How much fruit could Eve eat of and where?

Look at Genesis 3:1b. Notice how Satan twists and manipulates the truth to deceive Eve. How is the serpent described?

Read Genesis 3:6–7. What did Eve think she was gaining?

What was the promise from the serpent? Read Genesis 3:4b.

Since the Hebrew name for Eve actually means "living," isn't it ironic that the mother of the human race actually died spiritually when God had created her for life?

Have you ever sensed you were dying spiritually? What happened to you?

Satan will take a *little* bit of truth, combine it with Scripture—a half-truth is a lie—and attempt to distort reality, in order to deceive us. Satan even tried that with Jesus. Remember when Jesus was tempted for 40 days by Satan? Let's take a look at Jesus versus Satan.

> *Jesus, full of the Holy Spirit, returned from the Jordan and was led by the Spirit in the desert where for forty days he was tempted by the devil. He ate nothing during those days, and at the end of them he was hungry.*
>
> *The devil said to Him, "If you are the Son of God, tell this stone to become bread."*
>
> *Jesus answered, "It is written: 'Man does not live on bread alone.'"*
>
> *The devil led him up to a high place and showed him in an instant all the kingdoms of the world. And he said to him, "I will give you all their authority and splendor, for it has been given to me, and I can give it to anyone I want to. So if you worship me, it will all be yours."*
>
> *Jesus answered, "It is written: 'Worship the Lord your God and serve him only.'"*
>
> *The devil led him to Jerusalem and had him stand on the highest point of the temple. "If you are the Son of God," he said, "throw down yourself from here, for it is written, 'He will command his angels concerning you to guard you carefully: they will lift you up in their hands, so that you will not strike your foot against a stone.'"*
>
> *Jesus answered, "It says: 'Do not put the Lord your God to the test.'" When the devil had finished all this tempting, he left him until an opportune time.*
>
> —Luke 4:1–13

Who led Jesus into the desert and why?

Do you believe that Satan tempts us at opportune times as the Word says?

Explain and give an example:

Jesus was in the desert, hungry and thirsty, and Satan tempted Him with Scripture. Odd, isn't it? The devil knows the Word and knows how to use it to exploit our shame. We must know the Word and rely on the Holy Spirit to use God's truth on our behalf. Bad shame originated with Satan. However, the Word says that Jesus was led to the desert by the Holy Spirit.

Perhaps that is what God is doing in your life today. Maybe today is the day to let go of the bad shame and wear something other than Satan's garment of shame.

It is possible that God Himself has allowed you to have a "desert experience" and that it will ultimately strengthen your faith?

There *are* times when our sin—or others' abuse or neglect—brings us down to our knees in a second and rob us of our God-given self-esteem. Since the Fall, Satan has launched a full-forced attack—he tells us that *we* are a mistake. But God's Word, in so many ways, reveals that we are not. In fact, God tells us that He has redeemed us and has a plan or us, including working everything we experience together for our good.

What one thing that causes you shame do you believe that you can not let go?

Read what God has to say about His creation in us and His plans for us.

For it is by grace you have been saved, through faith—and this not from yourselves, it is the gift of God—not by works, so that no one can boast. For we are God's workmanship, created in Christ Jesus to do good works, which God prepared in advance for us to do.
—Ephesians 2:8–10

And we know that in all things God works for the good of those who love him, who have been called according to his purpose. For those God foreknew he also predestined to be conformed to the likeness of his Son, that he might be the firstborn among many brothers [and sisters]. And those he predestined, he also called; those he called, he also justified; those he justified, he also glorified. What, then, shall we say in response to this? If God is for us, who can be against us? He who did not spare his own Son, but gave him up for us all—how will he not also, along with him, graciously give us all things?
—Romans 8:28–32

Consider it pure joy, my brothers, whenever you face trials of many kinds, because you know that the testing of your faith develops perseverance. Perseverance must finish its work so that you may be mature and complete, not lacking anything.
—James 1:2–4

Thus, I believe the shame that originated in the Garden of Eden turned out to be a test. I am not saying that bad things happen to bad people. Just the opposite, really. When a person is abused in any way, it is a horrific encounter. However, that person must somehow cope with the shame of the abuse. The choice—being a victim or being a survivor—can make all the difference in the world.

We can either cling to God through Jesus Christ or shut Him out of our lives. We either wear that horrible garment of shame or we wear God's covering for us. God can turn our shame into His amazing glory. God Himself, venturing to this earth for Eve and Adam and, consequently, all of humankind, is the only one to beat Satan at his own game.

God's conviction—proper shame—comes from His Spirit revealing to us and convicting us of our sins according to Himself and His Word, when we reject His commands. And good shame can help bring about our healing.

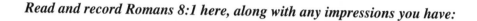

Recall a time where you felt shame. Was the Holy Spirit convicting you or was it the bad shame Satan tried to use to condemn you?

Read and record Romans 8:1 here, along with any impressions you have:

Satan tells us such things as:
• *You are nothing but a sorry person.*
• *You are such a disappointment.*

Does this verse from Romans help you to dispel Satan's lies? How?

How can we combat Satan when he barrages us with immense shame tactics?

Have you ever considered that God is allowing you to be led into the desert by Himself, resulting in testing by Satan and his knowledge of Scripture?

Do you counterattack Satan with Scripture, as Jesus did while He was in the desert? Why or why not?

Soul Disease and Cleansing

It was not until their eyes *"were opened and they realized they were naked"* (v. 7a) that they felt the shame of their sin. Adam and Eve must have felt tremendous shame after believing a lie from one of the most beautiful and craftiest of creatures. *What would God say or do to them now?* Adam and Eve made coverings for their bodies. The perfect relationship that they had enjoyed was embedded deeply with horrible shame. But we will take a look at and see how our gracious heavenly Father responds to their disobedience.

Genesis 3:10 reads, "He answered, 'I heard you in the garden, and I was afraid because I was naked; so I hid.'" *Why are Adam and Eve afraid of God?*

Why did God ask them this question that He already knew the answer to, since He knows everything?: "Have you eaten from the tree that I commanded you not to eat from?" (Genesis 3:11).

Does God know everything about you?

Proper shame should cause us to admit to sin, wrongdoing, or a mistake. God's Word in the New Testament tells believers, *"If we confess our sins, he is faithful and just and will forgive our sins and purify us from all unrighteousness"* (1 John 1:9). Biblically, good shame seems to indicate that conviction by the Holy Spirit is a blessing, to cleanse our souls.

What do you think keeps us from immediately coming to God rather than running to Him when we sin or have been sinned against?

You may wish to share your thoughts on how difficult it can be to come to God in these instances. The Bible says that this sharing is appropriate. *"Therefore confess your sins to each other and pray for each other so that you may be healed. The prayer of a righteous man is powerful and effective"* (James 5:16).

Read Psalm 34:5. What does God promise to do for us if we look to Him?

May those who hope in you
   not be disgraced because of me,
   O Lord, the LORD Almighty;
   may those who seek you
   not be put to shame because of me,
   O God of Israel.
For I endure scorn for your sake,
   and shame covers my face.
I am a stranger to my brothers,
   an alien to my own mother's sons;
—Psalm 34:5

Record your responses in the space provided:

What is God telling you through His Word?

These verses seem to indicate that we should look to the Lord in order not to feel the wrong type of shame. Yet, in the course of human history—and in our individual lives—it is easy to see that people choose to do the opposite. On day two of this week, we will look at why this is so and how God views this.

WEEK 1 • DAY 2
THE CONTROL OF HIDING

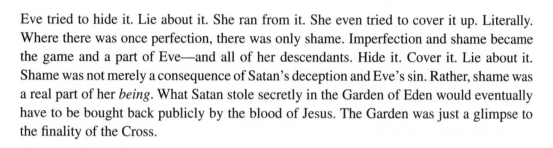

Then the man and his wife heard the sound of the Lord God as he was walking in the garden in the cool of the day, and they hid from the Lord God among the trees of the garden. But the Lord God called to the man, "Where are you?"
—Genesis 3:8

Eve tried to hide it. Lie about it. She ran from it. She even tried to cover it up. Literally. Where there was once perfection, there was only shame. Imperfection and shame became the game and a part of Eve—and all of her descendants. Hide it. Cover it. Lie about it. Shame was not merely a consequence of Satan's deception and Eve's sin. Rather, shame was a real part of her *being*. What Satan stole secretly in the Garden of Eden would eventually have to be bought back publicly by the blood of Jesus. The Garden was just a glimpse to the finality of the Cross.

Read Genesis 3:1–3. Have you ever been exploited by someone whom you thought was trustworthy? How did it make you feel?

Were you fooled by the person's appearance?

Read Genesis 3:1 again. It is crucial for us to continue to remember that Satan (appearing as a serpent) is craftier than all the other animals God made (v. 1).

Express your feelings about being taken for a ride or deceived in some matter, recently or long ago.

God's Word tells us, *"And no wonder, for Satan himself masquerades as an angel of light. It is not surprising then, if his servants masquerade as servants of righteousness"* (2 Corinthians 11:14–15).

How does this relate to what happened in the Garden of Eden?

Sometimes the people who seem to be the best looking, friendliest, and the most accommodating are actually wolves in sheep's clothing. *"Watch out for false prophets. They come to you in sheep's clothing but inwardly they are ferocious wolves"* (Matthew 7:15). *"His speech is smooth as butter, yet war is in his heart; his words are more soothing than oil, yet they are drawn swords"* (Psalm 55:20–22).

What does this truth from God mean to you personally? Can you give an example that you would share with others?

What one thing did Eve desire when the serpent came to her? See Genesis 3:5.

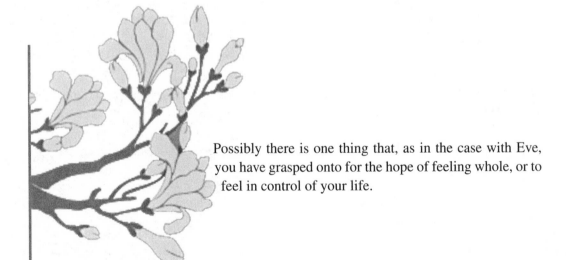

Possibly there is one thing that, as in the case with Eve, you have grasped onto for the hope of feeling whole, or to feel in control of your life.

If that is the case, what is it and how does it or did it make you feel after giving in to this temptation?

I've often wondered whether Eve felt cheated by God and that was the reason Satan was able to deceive her. Maybe she thought, *How rude of God not to let me eat of that one tree...He's holding back on me.* Eve wanted everything; not just the leftovers.

Have you ever felt that way? Please explain here:

Is there one particular thing that brings you more bad shame than anything else?

Think about it. Even if you were abused by someone else in some manner, in what ways does Satan tempt you to attempt to cover that up? Eating disorder? Workaholism? Substance abuse? Something else?

Yet, the truth is that God sees our shame, doesn't He?

Eve didn't merely tremble when she heard God walking in the garden at dusk that fateful day. She was physically, emotionally, and spiritually terrified to the point of never wanting to see her Creator face to face again. Therefore, when God asked her what she had done, Eve, I imagine, lowered her shame-ridden, darting eyes and gave what she had never given before: an excuse as her out. *"The serpent deceived me and I ate"* (Genesis 3:13b).

Do you sometimes conveniently lie to cover up the truth from being known? How does it make you feel?

Do you defend whatever it is to the death, or have you confessed it to God?

Record your response to Isaiah 40:5a: "And the glory of the Lord will be revealed."

What do you think God is revealing to you now about confessing your shame to Him or what one area of shame has God revealed to you recently?

Satan had deceived Eve. She immediately despised not only herself, but also what she had done and especially what she did afterward—cowering by the bushes in the darkness of sin and shame instead of walking in the light of the truth with her Creator, hand-in-hand through the garden.

In that moment, Eve had traded who God had perfectly created her to be. She had bought the ultimate lie of all time; that she was defective to her very core, despite having been created by and walking in a perfect relationship with God. Her original true identity as one made in God's image had been stolen. She had traded that identity for a false identity Satan had sold to her.

Do you feel flawed in a particular area of your life? What can you do to change that lie/shame?

How consistent are we at doing what Paul said God desired for us to do?: "Rather, clothe yourselves with the Lord Jesus Christ, and do not think about how to gratify the desires of the sinful nature" (Romans 13:14).

Did Eve give in to gratify her sinful nature?

In what ways do we resemble Eve? Be specific:

WEEK 1 • DAY 3
THE CLOTHING OF EVE

The Lord God made garments of skin for Adam and his wife and clothed them.
—Genesis 3:21

It was a simple choice. Jesus chose to keep poor humanity company while here on earth. *Poor* as viewed in the eyes of many in the world—outcasts. Orphans. Children. The hungry. The naked. The sexually impure. The emotionally unstable. Quite bluntly, Jesus consistently chose to spend His time with the ones whom respectable society would never have deemed worthy. That is, worthy in the eyes of the world.

Jesus did not merely shout from heaven to say, "I understand," but rather entered into our marred picture. Jesus came to be right here with us, helping to pick us up when we fall. Look at the compassion when God's Word says, *"The Lord God made garments of skin for Adam and his wife and clothed them."* He provided a solution for our shame. He clothed His children through a sacrifice—by the fur of an animal. There had to be blood, an animal's, in order to cover humankind. God's chosen sacrifice foreshadowed another sacrifice. The fall and aftermath foreshadowed the finality of Good Friday.

Two other men, both criminals, were also led out with him to be executed. When they came to the place called the Skull, there they crucified him, along with the criminals—one on his right, the other on his left. Jesus said, "Father, forgive them, for they do not know what they are doing." And they divided up his clothes by casting lots.

The people stood watching, and the rulers even sneered at him. They said, "He saved others; let him save himself if he is the Christ of God, the Chosen One."

The soldiers also came up and mocked him. They offered him wine vinegar and said, "If you are the king of the Jews, save yourself."

There was a written notice above him, which read: THIS IS THE KING OF THE JEWS.

One of the criminals who hung there hurled insults at him: "Aren't you the Christ? Save yourself and us!"

But the other criminal rebuked him. "Don't you fear God," he said, "since you are under the same sentence?

We are punished justly, for we are getting what our deeds deserve. But this man has done nothing wrong."

Then he said, "Jesus, remember me when you come into your kingdom."

Jesus answered him, "I tell you the truth, today you will be with me in paradise."
—Luke 2:32–43

In your own words, explain the parallel example of the fall and God's animal sacrifice to that of Jesus's sacrifice on the Cross:

"For He has clothed me with garments of salvation and arrayed me in a robe of righteousness" (Isaiah 61:10*b*). **Notice that God uses the plural noun of** *garments* **of salvation. Why might God use the plural sense of the word garment? Does not God totally clothe us as He did Eve and Adam?**

Galatians 3:27 reads, "For all of you who were baptized into Christ have clothed yourselves with Christ." **What does this mean to you?**

Do we run and hide as Eve and Adam did? I don't know about you, but I run and hide sometimes from God because I am afraid of Him knowing what I've done. I don't merely feel the shame of what I have *done*, but rather, I feel shame for who I think I *am*. I simply don't *make* a mistake; I feel that I *am* a mistake. That is Satan's voice that tells us to cover up our shortcomings according to his way and to try to fix ourselves.

Instead, God wants us to run to Him, *Abba,* our Daddy, and jump into His arms—regardless of that which is shameful that has happened to us at the hands of another person or regardless of what we have done. We can either embrace Satan's shame, or hold out our hearts and lives to Jesus for life incidents that are not according to His plan.

List as many sources of shame that you hold onto today as a result of shame by another person/persons. (You will need to discern carefully who to share this with in any one-on-one or group discussion):

Why don't we wear God's garments of salvation and righteousness and fully step out into the healing light of Christ, instead of slithering around in the darkness of shame?

Read and write out Romans 13:14:

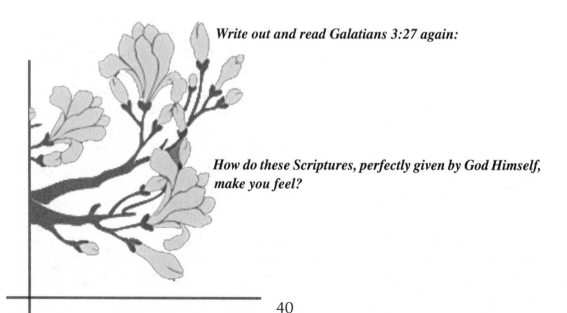

Write out and read Galatians 3:27 again:

How do these Scriptures, perfectly given by God Himself, make you feel?

Week 1 • Day 4
Clothing Others

When he had said this, Jesus called in a loud voice, "Lazarus, come out!" The dead man came out, his hands and feet wrapped with strips of linen, and a cloth around his face. Jesus said to them, "Take off the grave clothes and let him go."
—John 11:43–44

Have you ever thought a situation was impossible but then saw a miracle performed? God tells us the story of how Jesus miraculously brought His close friend Lazarus back from the dead.

Can you imagine the crowd that milled around, waiting for Jesus to visit and give His condolences to Mary and Martha? Jesus waited four days in order to nullify anyone's doubt that Lazarus was dead. In fact, three days after death was the limit to wait before burial, but Christ waited four days so that their was no confusion that Lazarus was dead.

Now a man named Lazarus was sick. He was from Bethany, the village of Mary and her sister Martha. This Mary, whose brother Lazarus now lay sick, was the same one who poured perfume on the Lord and wiped his feet with her hair. So the sisters sent word to Jesus, "Lord, the one you love is sick." When he heard this, Jesus said, "This sickness will not end in death. No, it is for God's glory so that God's Son may be glorified through it." Jesus loved Martha and her sister and Lazarus. Yet when he heard that Lazarus was sick, he stayed where he was two more days.
On his arrival, Jesus found that Lazarus had already been in the tomb for four days. Bethany was less than two miles from Jerusalem, and many Jews had come to Martha and Mary to comfort them in the loss of their brother.
—John 11:1–6, 7, 17–18

After Jesus arrived in Bethany and went to Lazarus's tomb—"Jesus wept" (John 11:35). It is the shortest sentence in all of God's Word, and yet its significance cannot be measured. Not merely crying, but deep mourning with emotions. The Greek word for "wept" here means deep emotional distress. This verse testifies to God becoming flesh in the person of Jesus. He truly is *Emmanuel*, God with us. Perhaps Jesus wept so much because He deeply loved Lazarus. Two words: one life, I imagine that Jesus had spent many days with Lazarus, Mary, and Martha. They had talked, broken bread together, and lived passionately in relationship.

41

Perhaps another reason Jesus wept was to show us His humanness. He knew He was about to raise Lazarus from physical death. But He still wept. He still felt the way we do when we lose someone close to our hearts. We are but fragile instruments and these two words demonstrate Christ's humanity,

> *When Jesus saw her weeping, and the Jews who had come along with her also weeping, he was deeply moved in spirit and troubled. "Where have you laid him?" he asked.*
>
> *"Come and see, Lord," they replied.*
>
> *Jesus wept.*
>
> *Then the Jews said, "See how he loved him!"*
>
> —John 11:35–36

He wept, too, because of people's sin and shame and His love for humanity (John 11:41).

Next, Jesus showed His omnipotence. Jesus is God and He knew that He would be raising Lazarus from the dead.

Then why did He wait so long?

> *So they took away the stone. Then Jesus looked up and said, "Father, I thank you that you have heard me. I knew that you always hear me, but I said this for the benefit of the people standing here that they may believe that you sent me."*
>
> —John 11:41–42

This miracle was for the doubters. Sure, some thought Jesus was the Messiah, but there were many doubters.

I believe that God also allowed a crowd in Bethany because Jesus wanted *people* to take the grave clothes off Lazarus. Read John 11:43–44. It was easy for Jesus to raise Lazarus from the dead miraculously. Why didn't Jesus take off the strips of linen grave clothes too? Surely He could have done this.

Why did Jesus command others to "take off the grave clothes and let him go" (v. 44*b*)?

Do we as Christians have the burden or obligation to remove other people's "grave clothes", that is, the hindrances in their lives?

Jesus commanded the onlookers to take away Lazarus's grave clothes. When you help someone in need, is it an obligation as a believer or is it a privilege?

What are your "grave clothes"? What keeps you from living the life God has for you— and do you need help to remove these impediments?

All of us have hang-ups or areas of our lives that impede us from living the life God has called us to live. His Word challenges, *"let us throw off everything that hinders us"* (Hebrews 12:1). We can either let others help us along the way, or we can remain embittered, resentful, and "dead" to the world.

In many churches, when a newborn is dedicated, the entire congregation says they will do all they can to help that baby flourish in the church and society. We owe each other more and no less to help when some person is drowning in a sea of depression, experiencing the aftermath of rape, sexual and emotional abuse, abortion, or another life crisis. It is a privilege and honor we have to uphold the standards of God to each and every member of the church, as well as to extend this help outside the church by God's guidance. We can either turn away or we can be patient and help take some of those grave clothes off.

Jesus pointed to this practice in His own death. There is no better example of this form of care than when Jesus told John to take care of His mother at His death.

When Jesus saw his mother there and the disciple whom he loved standing nearby, he said to his mother, "Dear woman, here is your son." And to the disciple "Here is your mother." From that time on, this disciple took her into his home.
—John 19:26–27

Why do you think Jesus chose John to take care of His mother after His death?

What would you have done if you had been in Jesus's place?

God's Word tells us that the Romans took away Jesus's clothes. *"When they had crucified him they divided up his clothes by casting lots"* (Matthew 27:35). It's ironic because we have been "clothed" in Him, though He lay naked on the cross. Even in death, Jesus covered us with His life.

Begin to memorize and reflect on Hebrews 12:2: *"Let us fix our eyes on Jesus, the author and perfecter of our faith, who for the joy set before him endured the cross, scorning its shame.* Don't take my word regarding shame...take God's.

Write out Isaiah 61:10–11:

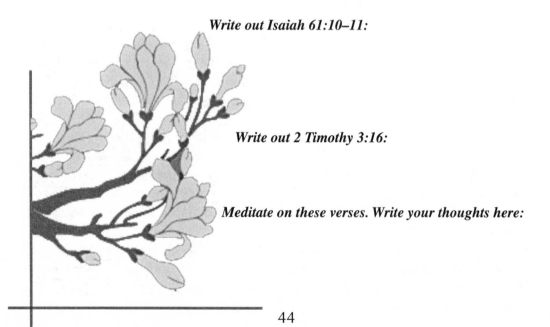

Write out 2 Timothy 3:16:

Meditate on these verses. Write your thoughts here:

WEEK 1 • DAY 5
THE CHOICE OF CONTROL

For He chose us before the creation of the world.
—Ephesians 1:4

Control is a two-edged sword. On one hand, we have a choice in some actions we can take. On the other hand, some situations are out of our control. At times we are faced with life-altering events. Even Job came to understand: *"Do you know how God controls the clouds..."* (Job 37:15).

I will never forget getting a phone call from a friend who told me my close friend and prayer partner had been diagnosed with cancer. Martha, about four months pregnant, was given a choice none of us would fathom to make: abort the baby or go through chemotherapy and hope the baby would not be too badly deformed. Martha told me that it was an easy choice. She would take chemo, baby and all. Through the months that we spent together and prayed together, Martha knew she wasn't in control of the outcome. What she *could* control was her ability to pray and trust God with the outcome. After six grueling months of chemotherapy, Martha delivered a perfectly healthy four-pound baby girl. Martha died five months later after delivering the miracle baby.

Can you remember a time when you felt that you were in complete control? How did it make you feel?

Now what about another time where you had zero control? How did you bear it?

Did you experience bad shame during this time? How?

Let's not forget about taking off each others' grave clothes. Do you need help?

After Martha died, I needed help. The smallest thing would make me cry. I tried my best to move on but got stuck. Had it not been for friends and family, I never would have made it.

We all have choices, such as what to eat, where to shop, what not to buy, and so on, but we are fragile creatures. Sometimes the events in our lives bring us loss of control, and with it shame. Rather than fighting for control, we need to remember that we have a sovereign Creator and to give up our lack of control to a benevolent God.

Do you agree or disagree with that last statement? Why or why not?

Satan came to Eve and not Adam to tempt them. Why do you think this was?

Since Eve was deceived, her shameful consequences are found in Genesis 3:16 *"Your desire will be for your husband and he will rule over you."* Eve not only had control over her husband, but also she would endure spiritual, emotional, and physical pain.

When doctors diagnosed my friend Martha as having lymphoma cancer, I was shocked. Not Martha. My Martha. My prayer partner. That was without a doubt one of the most uncontrollable moments in my life. Right then and there I had a choice to make about a situation I had no control over. As I sped over to the hospital that first day, and I decided then and there that I would stay with her through thick and thin by turning closer to God. No matter how bad it got, I would be there for her.

God drew me to Himself; I was amazed as He poured out His strength—His control—on His child repeatedly! Late one night, I saw Martha witness to a doctor, nurse, and anybody who entered her room. Her spiritual insight was that we are all terminal; we simply don't know it yet, and that she did. While Martha wasted away physically, I saw Jesus as never before.

God covered Martha and she delivered her baby daughter—a miracle.... Martha witnessed though she wasn't coherent....

I saw, in essence, Christ poured out as a cup of cold water on a hot August afternoon. The verse that allowed me to share in the experience is Philippians 2:17–18.

But even if I am being poured out like a drink offering
on the sacrifice and service coming from your faith, I
am glad and rejoice with all of you. So you too should be glad and
rejoice with me.
—Philippians 2:17–18

Though I had begged God to take me and not her, since I felt she were a much better believer than I was, God said no. If I had walked away from Martha in the end, as many people seem to choose to do in these very difficult experiences, I would have missed seeing Christ as never before.

I miss my friend terribly, but have come to learn that the Word of God is true. We can't control what happens to us in this life, but we can choose to draw closer to God in an intimate, sustaining relationship through Jesus Christ.

Have you ever seen a life poured out like a drink offering?

If you are experiencing this study in a group, you will have an opportunity to share with others, or watch for an opportunity God provides to use one of your own desert experiences to encourage someone else to release their shame and any other area of need to Him.

What is a desert experience you would share with others?

Author C. S. Lewis in *The Problem of Pain* describes pain as "God's megaphone." If that is the case, then I guess I am deaf. I would never have traded the intimacy I shared with Martha for anything in the world, except for one thing: for her to be healed. It has been many years since Martha died, and I still cry at time as though it happened yesterday.

I prayed for her healing. It didn't come. I prayed for the rapture to come. It didn't. Then I saw God's hand moving. Not in one day, one month, or one year, but years later now. When it is all said and done, we all have choices. Martha made her choice. I made mine. I felt no shame when Martha died. I felt sort of relieved. Relieved that she was no longer in pain. No longer hooked up to machines. No longer suffering. God drew me to what was flowing out of her in her final days. I saw glory—God's glory—and no shame.

THE FRIENDSHIP TEARS

"He will swallow up death forever. The Sovereign Lord
will wipe away the tears."
—Isaiah 25:8

I come to You with
unashamed friendship tears to weep.
You never tell me to stem them,
only to pour them at Your feet.

She was a light down here
for just a short while.
I never dreamed the race she would run
on behalf of heaven's mile.

Tenderness, touch, and trust
were ours indeed to share.
You freed my soul to love
as it was brokenly laid bare.

Many years ago I asked You
what friendship was all about.
You opened heaven's graceful gate
and whispered Martha's name with evidence of a shout.

So deaf did I become
as I begged for time to keep.

"This my precious child is proof of My love for you,
because I have given you freedom with friendship tears to weep."

—*Deb Vanderslice*

There was no shame at all as Martha died. Only God's amazing glory captivated me. When everything failed her physically and mentally—her soul laid bare—in her Spirit, others saw Jesus. What once had been hidden more than 2,000 years ago shone—the beautiful light of Jesus's witness in a world full of darkness. *"He... brings hidden things to light"* (Job 28:11). Maybe we at times believe we have no choices, but I say we do. Even in the worst-case scenarios. We can either choose shame or choose glory; darkness or the light.

What has God been gently urging you to do or to not do? Do you have a choice to make? What will it be? Remember, if it is Satan's form of shame, it comes as a lie from hell.

My Prayer

Dear Lord, I confess my sins and those done to me. I know that You are in control of my life and the tapestry You are perfecting for me. Give me the help and fortitude to keep stepping out of shame and into Your truth. Help me to run to You, not walk, whenever I feel shame from the evil one. You alone make me worthy. Give me the heart knowledge to change my wrong perceptions of You, how You feel about me, and Your control in my life. Amen.

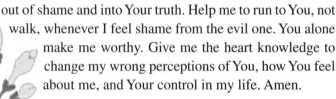

Your Prayer

PART 2

Shameless

Week 2

Standing Tall with Broken Promises
Tamar

And so Jesus also suffered outside the city gates to make the people holy through his own blood.
—Hebrews 13:12

This week, we are going to focus on the first of the five women listed in Jesus's genealogy. This example, the relationship between Tamar and her father-in-law, Judah, and his sons deals with the shame of their broken vows and promises.

In the course of Tamar's story, we also see the deception on her part in her need to become pregnant. However, God keeps His commitments. God brings blessing out of shame. He is faithful to all His promises, and the Levirate marriage custom was no exception. God is faithful because of His righteousness and He cannot deny Himself. *"God is not a man that he should lie"* (Numbers 23:19*a*).

Week 2 • Day 1
Outside the City Limits

Judah got a wife for Er, his firstborn and her name was Tamar.
—Deuteronomy 25:6–7

An unlikely source. An unstable candidate. A compromising woman. God could have chosen a less-complicated woman. He could have chosen a more-sanctified woman. He could have chosen a less-conniving woman. But He didn't. God chose a complex, stubborn, and sexually deceitful woman named Tamar to become the first of the women listed in the genealogy of Christ. The entire premise on which hinges Tamar's role as a direct ancestor of Christ revolves around an Old Testament Israelite custom called the Levirate marriage law. The Latin word *levir* actually means "brother-in-law," which is exactly what the custom entailed.

It was against Jewish tradition to marry outside the bounds of Jewish law.

No one born of a forbidden marriage nor any of his descendants may enter the assembly of the Lord, even down to the tenth generation. No Ammonite or Moabite or any of his descendants may enter the assembly of the Lord, even down to the tenth generation.
—Deuteronomy 23:2–3

Now look at what Judah did. *"Judah got a wife for Er, his firstborn and her name was Tamar. But Er, Judah's firstborn, was wicked in the Lord's sight; so the Lord put him to death"* (Deuteronomy 25:6–7). Judah definitely knew the Levirate marriage law, but chose instead for his son to marry a Gentile. Thus, Tamar married a Jewish man, Er, even though she herself was not.

When and if a brother died, it also was customary for a brother-in-law to step in to fulfill the Law.

If brothers are living together and one of them dies without a son, his widow must not marry outside the family. Her husband's brother shall take her and marry her and fulfill the duty of a brother-in-law to her. The first son she bears shall carry on the name of the dead brother so that his name will not be blotted out from Israel.
—Deuteronomy 25:5–6

What does 1 Chronicles 2:3–4 say?

It is interesting to note that Judah's wife had not been an Israelite either.

While Tamar was a product of an outside heritage, Eve was created by God's very own hands. Eve's direct lineage, which takes place in the Garden of Eden, is one of perfection, while Tamar's originated in sin. Eve lived in the Garden, but eventually outside of God's plan, while Tamar was born outside the parameters of God's people, the Israelites, but lived inside God's domain.

Reading Leviticus 4:*a*, 12, 21*b*, we see another symbolic measure that proves sacrifices took place outside the Israeli camp. *"The priest...must take* [a bull] *outside the camp. This is the sin offering for the community."*

While Eve's atonement apparently took place inside the Garden of Eden, blood sacrifices during Tamar's life took place outside the camp. How ironic that God specifically uses this to demonstrate His love for us: that He offered up His only Son as the perfect sacrifice for us while we were outsiders to Him. *"When we were utterly helpless, Christ came at just the right time and died for us sinners"* (Romans 5:6 NLT).

Will God not go outside the perceived norm to execute His divine plan?

God demonstrates early on in the genealogy of Christ, that He will, in Tamar's heritage, choose to go outside the Israelites and their laws.

What does this represent to you when you consider God's desire to free humankind from sin and shame?

God does indeed go outside the norm in Tamar's case, to fulfill His purposes. God goes outside the box and chooses a Gentile woman to carry the line of Jesus, when He could have allowed her to go barren.

What else do we know about Tamar, aside from the fact that we know she is an outsider, or Canaanite woman? We know that her husband, Er, descended from a forbidden union, and died, as shown in 1 Chronicles 2:3–4, died because he was evil in the Lord's eyes. We know Tamar then expected her brother-in-law to step in to fulfill the Levirate marriage law.

Then we read that yet another of Judah's son failed to obey God's law.

> *Then Judah said to Onan, lie with your brother's wife and fulfill your duty to her as a brother-in-law to produce offspring for your brother. But Onan knew that the offspring would not be his; so whenever he lay with his brother's wife, he spilled his semen on the ground to keep from producing offspring for his brother. What he did was wicked in the Lord's sight; so He put him to death also.*
> —Genesis 3:8–10

Why do you think Onan did not fulfill his obligation to Tamar and, overall, to his family?

Have you ever expected something important to happen and it didn't? What kind of emotions did you have once your expectations fell through?

Can you imagine the gamut of emotions that Tamar must have felt? Shock at the death of her first husband. Hope for the future with her brother-in-law. Disgust with Onan for not following through with his sexual obligation. Shock again at the death of Onan. The shame of barrenness as her worth was directly tied to her ability to give birth to a son to carry on Judahite lineage. Could it possibly get any worse?

Alone and frightened, a desperate hope was all Tamar had left. That is exactly what her father-in-law, Judah, gave her, though he actually thought there was no hope at all for her.

> *Judah then said to his daughter-in-law Tamar, "Live as a widow in your father's house until my son Shelah grows up." For he thought, "He may die too, just like his brothers." So Tamar went to live in her father's house.*
> —Genesis 38:11

Why did Judah lie to Tamar?

What was Judah afraid would happen?

There it is, plain and simple: hope—a two-edged sword. Hope can give you the wings to soar and zest to keep on living, while the loss of hope can bring you down and devastate you. *"Hope deferred makes the heart sick, but a longing fulfilled is a tree of life"* (Proverbs 13:12). Judah never intended to give Shelah to Tamar when this young son grew up. Having lost two wicked sons, Judah probably was terrified of losing a third son. Funny, isn't it? Judah ignored the Levirate marriage law in hopes that his son would not die, while fulfilling it could actually have brought life to his heritage.

What hope do you have in God?

What fears do you have that, if you succumb to them, might interfere with what God has purposed for your life?

Week 2 • Day 2
The Faithful Daughter-in-Law

He is the Rock, his works are perfect, and all his ways are just. A faithful God who does no wrong, upright and just is he.
—Deuteronomy 32:4

Tamar had trusted Judah completely. She expected her father-in-law to be faithful to his word and God's law. She left for her father's house based on what Judah promised, though he had lied. Tamar went at once and was obedient to Judah's wishes. Only, Judah had other plans. He broke the promise of the Levirate marriage law as he had broken God's command not to marry outside the Israelite people. Judah stood in a fatherly role to Tamar and yet He did not keep His promise to her.

Eve traded a truth for a lie, Judah traded in lies, while Tamar believed a lie.

Have you ever lied to cover up something, only to find out it would have been better to tell the truth?

Was Tamar obedient to her word?

Remember, Tamar was an outsider, a Canaanite woman. Had she done anything wrong as far as you can see?

When we think of Tamar and her circumstances, we probably can relate. Being lied to? A broken promise? An unexpected loss? Maybe the death of a loved one? Perhaps an unforeseen health problem?

I will never forget the hot July summer afternoon when I was called to go to the hospital because Martha was fighting for her life. I remember asking myself, *Where are all the adults? When are some older adults going to arrive and get rid of the panic?* It then dawned on me: *We are the adults.* It was overwhelming; I had no control over my friend's life.

How do you think Tamar held on to hope for so long, though she had no control?

Day after day. Month after month. Year after year. Previous to that moment in the hospital with my friend, I had undergone ten bile-duct surgeries in a two-year period. Again, there had been no control over my sickness.

When my husband filed for divorce, I had felt the same loss of control. Surely there was something that could be done! But there wasn't. I was left feeling damaged.

Have you ever felt damaged in some form or fashion? I think that is how Tamar felt. Numb disbelief. Shock. Anger. Denial. Finally, acceptance. Tamar had been promised a future husband. She hoped and trusted in her father-in-law.

Again, when we try to fix our shameful and hurting situations ourselves or trust other people to do so, sometimes matters get worse. I have had that experience. And I don't know about you, but sometimes waiting for God gets old. I want things now. Done yesterday. Many times I have taken matters into my own hands, only to find out words should have been left unsaid, and actions not taken. Haven't we all gone outside of God's will at least once in order to accommodate our timing? Tamar did. We have.

> *After a long time Judah's wife, the daughter of Shua, died. When Judah had recovered from his grief, he went up to Timnah, to the men who were shearing his sheep, and his friend Hirah the Adullamite went with him.*
>
> *When Tamar was told, "Your father-in-law is on his way to Timnah to shear his sheep," she took off her widow's clothes, covered herself with a veil to disguise herself, and then sat down at the entrance to Enaim, which is on the road to Timnah. For she saw that, though Shelah had now grown up, she had not been given to him as his wife.*
> —Genesis 38:13–14

Maybe you are ashamed because of illicit sexual behavior, substance abuse, depression, or other issues. Let's keep on reading about Tamar.

She hid her face and *"sat down at the entrance to Enaim"* (Genesis 38:14*b*). Prostitutes customarily positioned themselves on the road, especially at the entrance to a city. In a desperate act, Tamar traded her hope for shame. She felt she *must* produce a son. I imagine she decided somewhere along the way that the Hebrew God was silent, aloof, and oblivious to her predicament.

What do you see here that Eve and Tamar have in common? List as many similarities as you can:

Imagine the range of emotions Tamar felt as she took matters into her own hands and describe what she did?

Tamar hid, covering herself to conceal her true identity. This is the same action that Eve had taken in the garden. Both women struggled with a common denominator: *shame*. Notice that both women hid from the One who sustained them, and opted for taking matters into their own hands.

Tamar hid from the one person who could redeem her life, yet she chose to take matters into her own hands—as we often do, despite the fact that we have a loving heavenly Father who wants to deliver us from shame. He is the same gracious God today as He was yesterday and will be forever. *"The Lord God made garments of skin for Adam and his wife and clothed them"* (Genesis 3:21).

WEEK 2 • DAY 3
A HOPE AND A FUTURE

"For I know the plans I have for you," declares the Lord,
"plans to prosper you and not to harm you, plans to
give you hope and a future"
—Jeremiah 29:11

Don't you know that Tamar had counted the days until she could become a wife again and a mother? Each year, the time had grown closer to fulfilling this longing. But, as much as she had hoped, her future dream had died a slow death.

Shelah was well old enough for her. Then one day, she had had enough. Since her father-in-law was nearby, she decided to take the Levirate marriage law into her own hands. Sin or no sin. Shame or no shame. She put away her mourning clothes and slipped into a prostitute's garb. Had Tamar set the trap? Most definitely.

Have you ever done anything to trick someone in a manipulative event? Have you fooled someone into doing something they didn't know about?

What kind of sin is Tamar willing to risk and why do you think she is so desperate?

God is the opposite of what Tamar thought to be true. While Judah had not been faithful to his word, God is always faithful. While Judah proved to be dishonest, God proved to be the Truth...true to all His promises despite human beings' failures, including Tamar's, as she would find out.

When Judah saw her, he thought she was a prostitute, for she had covered her face.
Not realizing that she was his daughter-in-law, he went over to her by the roadside
and said, "Come now, let me sleep with you."
—Genesis 38:15–16

After Judah approached Tamar for sex, she asked him what he would give her if she were to sleep with him. During biblical times, Jewish men wore a seal that was used to sign clay documents and the men would wear it around their neck on a cord.

What might a modern-day seal be in terms of identification?

"Will you give me something as a pledge until you send it?" she asked. He said, "What pledge should I give you?" "Your seal and its cord, and the staff in your hand," she answered. So he gave them to her and slept with her, and she became pregnant by him. After she left, she took off her veil and put on her widow's clothes again.
—Genesis 38:18–19

Though Judah had offered Tamar a goat, that was not good enough for her, and with good reason. Tamar wanted a *telltale* pledge, so Judah agreed.

What was the significance of asking for his staff, seal, and cord?

What one piece of identification defines your existence today?

Let's look at Tamar's actions a little more closely. Tamar had one chance to become pregnant by her father-in-law. If she were to conceive, she would have had to know the exact time and number of days she would be able to conceive. That takes planning on her part; deceit to dress up as a prostitute; and duplicity to ensure his staff, cord, and seal.

Although we may be appalled that a daughter-in-law and a father-in-law created an offspring, let us look to what

64

Tamar endured to try to see that Judah fulfilled the Levirate marriage law.

- Tamar was patient at first. Day after day. Month after month. Year after year.
- Tamar was also trusting. She took Judah at his word when he said that Shelah would be her husband one day.
- Tamar was obedient when Judah told her to return to her father's house while waiting for Shelah to grow up.
- Tamar was courageous. She risked her life to play the part of the prostitute. In Old Testament times, the legal penalty for prostitution was being burned to death.

Have you ever felt or endured shame in order to gain something? Explain:

Have you ever felt so strongly about something that you were willing to risk your life for it? Explain:

While Tamar endured the shame of sexual intercourse with her father-in-law, she was, at best, a desperate woman in search of the fulfillment of a promise to her. Judah went on with his life until about three months later when word reached him that *"Tamar is guilty of prostitution, and as a result she is now pregnant"* (Genesis 38:24).

When we examine God's actions in this matter, we can be delighted to see that our lives, no matter what we have done in the past—of our own sinful doing or in retaliation to sin done to us by others—God is unfailing in His faithfulness. That was certainly the fact in Tamar's case.

Tamar's Hebrew name literally means "to be erect; a palm tree." She would overcome a broken promise, regardless of sin and her and others' shame, with God turning her shame into His own glory and causing her to stand tall in spite of everything, even herself.

WEEK 2 • DAY 4
TALK IS CHEAP

Then we will no longer be infants, tossed back and forth by the waves, and blown here and there by every wind of teaching and by the cunning and craftiness of men in their deceitful scheming.
—Ephesians 4:14–16

Judah's response to Tamar's pregnancy? *"Bring her out and have her burned to death!"* (Genesis 38:24*b*).

Describe what you believe were Tamar's feelings and emotions as she was brought out publicly by Judah for a sexual sin she had committed with him:

Judah does not even fathom his involvement with Tamar until she pulls the rabbit out of her hat. *"As Tamar was being brought out, she sent a message to her father-in-law. I am pregnant by the man who owns these"* (Genesis 38:25).

Look up Genesis 38:26–30. What is your stance on Judah?

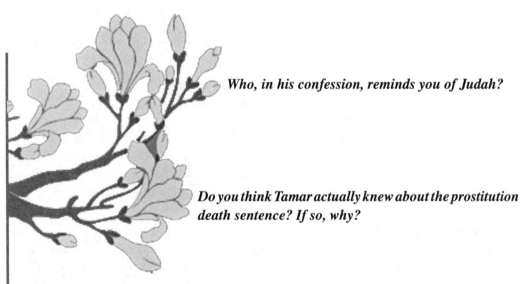

Who, in his confession, reminds you of Judah?

Do you think Tamar actually knew about the prostitution death sentence? If so, why?

It is interesting to note how God uses hiding in the midst of defining, or rather *refining* us—using our shame to change people. For example, at least five biblical people who were used mightily by God come to mind, but each had to go through the darkness or hiding before his or her life was refined by God.

- **There were Eve and Adam.** *Read Genesis 3:8 and record your findings here. As discussed in Week 1, why did they hide?*

What emotion do you think was most present?

- **There was Moses,** whom God hid at birth in the bulrushes of the Nile, and in the wilderness after he was run out of his exalted leadership in Egypt because he was found to have become a murderer.

By faith Moses' parents hid him for three months after he was born, because they saw he was no ordinary child...By faith Moses, when he had grown up, refused to be known as the son of Pharaoh's daughter. He chose to be mistreated along with the people of God rather than to enjoy the pleasures of sin for a short time. He regarded disgrace for the sake of Christ as of greater value than the treasures of Egypt.
—Hebrews 11:23–28

- **Jesus, Lord of the Universe, God Himself,** went into hiding. Jesus's heavenly Father had told His earthly "father" to hide Jesus in Egypt to escape Pharaoh's wrath in the beginning of His life. At Jesus's death, when darkness came over the land for three hours, was Satan snuffing out the Light of the world? No. God was in the process of taking Satan's plan and turning it into His plan of glory. *"It was now about the sixth hour, and darkness came over the whole land until the ninth hour for the sun stopped shining. And the curtain of the temple was torn in two"* (Luke 23:44–45). And on the third day, Later, Jesus was hidden in the tomb after He was crucified. But He arose, conquering sin, death, and the grave.

- **The Apostle Paul.** God transformed the zeal and zest Saul had for murdering Christians into the Apostle Paul's zeal for evangelism. But first, the darkness of Paul's temporary blindness came before the Light of the World could shine in his life. Paul was out of sight with Ananias for three days and God hid light from him in Saul's sightlessness while telling Saul His purposes and what Paul now would do with his life.

Eve, Moses, Jesus, Paul, Tamar, and others were at some point of time in the darkness. God used their hiding and brought them to the center of His Word publicly. *"If we had forgotten the name of our God…would not God have discovered it since he knows the secrets of the heart?"* (Psalm 44:20–21). Likewise, God in all His glory extends His long arm of grace to all who are ashamed. They weren't mere followers, but rather God used their shame to bring glory to Himself.

Tamar's story does not end after she disclosed Judah as father to her pregnancy. God graciously allows Tamar and Judah to be the parents of twin boys, Perez and Zerah. God allowed Tamar, as well as Judah, to be in the genealogy of Jesus. Tamar and Judah's son, Perez, eventually became head of the leading tribe in Judah—and, along with Tamar, an ancestor of Jesus.

A record of the genealogy of Jesus Christ the son of David, the son of Abraham: Abraham was the father of Isaac, Isaac the father of Jacob, Jacob the father of Judah and his brothers, Judah the father of Perez and Zerah, whose mother was Tamar, Perez the father of Hezron, Hezron the father of Ram…Thus there were fourteen generations in all from Abraham to David, fourteen from David to the exile to Babylon, and fourteen from the exile to the Christ.
—Matthew 1:1–3, 17

Isn't it ironic that, in shame, Tamar covered herself with a veil, and yet God uncovered that shame by exposing the truth of His promise through the Levirate marriage law, regardless of Tamar taking matters into her own hands?

In spite of Tamar's shame, God redeemed her hiding by displaying her in the covering of His glory in the direct lineage of Christ. A cunning, sexually immoral, and dishonest woman. A desperate woman. God chose Tamar, a tall, erect woman who had once stooped so low. When she

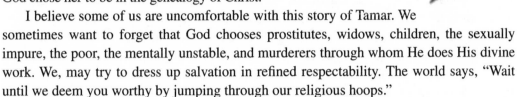

finally stepped out of her shame, God saw her standing as tall as her name implied. God did not allow Tamar to wallow in her shame.

Rather, He used that cunning to permit her to stand upright. God redeemed a broken promise born out of shame and turned it for His glory. Instead of remembering Tamar's sin and shame, God chose her to be in the genealogy of Christ.

I believe some of us are uncomfortable with this story of Tamar. We sometimes want to forget that God chooses prostitutes, widows, children, the sexually impure, the poor, the mentally unstable, and murderers through whom He does His divine work. We, may try to dress up salvation in refined respectability. The world says, "Wait until we deem you worthy by jumping through our religious hoops."

God says, *"Come now."*

Even though Tamar sinned in order to fulfill a marriage custom back in the Old Testament days, God still chose an outsider to be the first woman listed in the genealogy of Jesus.

Did Tamar's sins cause her to forfeit her role in the lineage of Jesus?

Did God put Tamar up on a shelf, never to be heard from again?

As women who have been shamed, either by our own sins or the sins of others, we see that God can, indeed, take a woman and her past and turn it into His glory. What God did for Tamar, He can do for us today.

Do you have your own story of how God has turned shame into His glory?

The story of Tamar waiting for her redemption reminds me of another story about a little old man who finally took a chance for freedom.

WEEK 2 • DAY 5
THAT OLD DAM

"Then you will know the truth, and the truth will set you free."
—John 8:32

After years and years the old dam broke. Many of the townspeople were stunned; their lives held captive by the overflow of water. Everyone was caught off guard. Except for Red.

Red was the little old man who fished everyday at that old dam. Whether it was 100 degrees in August and he had to battle the stifling summer heat with no hint of a hot breeze, or it was a snowy day in December, his frozen fingers wrapped around his old cane pole, Red went fishing just the same.

One day a town committee went to Red's home to ask him questions about that old dam. "Did you see it coming?"

"Did you know ahead of time? Is that why you stopped fishing?"

"We know you didn't know, otherwise you would have let the town folks know."

Red let them answer their own questions more or less, and he chuckled with his tongue in cheek. *Yes*, he thought to himself, *I'd seen it coming.* He'd known the dam would one day break, but he never knew exactly when.

Red didn't merely watch the red and white plastic cork bob up and down. He'd look around every now and then while fishing on that old dam. That dam he'd fished on for over 65 years.

The cracks in that old dam slowly expanded into larger ones. Day after day. Month after month. Year after year.

Red had grown to love that old dam, accustomed not to the fishing (for he never caught many fish) but rather he'd grown to love the solitude and peace that the sound of the water brought. The consistent ebb of its blue.

But one day the sound of the water began to change.

Yes, an architect could have inspected that old dam as the town committee had thought about…after the dam had given way.

It almost killed him that day. Not when the dam actually broke, but when he made the decision to stop going to that old dam.

There was something safe about that familiar place. That

familiar sight. That familiar smell. His familiar spot on that old dam.

Red though he didn't have a choice, but then again he did. Stay and be swept away or leave and mourn that old dam a little sooner.

The people in town just knew Red would die an old, old man fishing on that old dam. But they were wrong. It all changed for Red when the peculiarity of the water became predictable. It just wasn't the same for him on that old dam. He began to question the safety in the familiar.

If he left that old dam and his spot, he'd have to find something else to do with his time. That frightened Red. In fact, he almost chose to stay on the dam and be swept away.

But then one day Red did it. He left that old dam, his place marking the exact spot where the dam would later break.

It almost did kill him, leaving that old dam. But one day when the air was cool and light, the smell of the freshly cut lawn was sweet, and an easiness in the day was felt, Red began to see something that the old dam did not offer him. A chance to live. To experience new things. New sounds. New sights. His spot changed the day he left that old dam.

It never ceased to amaze Red when he was out and about in his life how many people said it must be killing him to not be fishing at the dam.

But Red would always answer this question by putting his weathered hands deep within his pockets, poking around his sparse spare change. While the thought of the old dam breaking was wreaking havoc on the town, Red would think to himself, *the flood would allow me the chance of a lifetime.* That which he had thought would kill him actually saved his life.

And so it was OK when the townspeople laid old Red to rest in the cemetery under the blooming Bradford pear.

They thought old Red had died of a broken heart. Oh, if only they knew the truth about his heart...giving out because of the fullness of life he was living.

But it was OK with Red, because he knew the truth about that old dam.

—Deb Vanderslice

What caused Old Red to finally get off that old dam and did he listen to others or did he do it humbly by himself?

How does this story relate to Tamar finally breaking free from the chains of her lost hope?

How are Red and Tamar alike and how are they different?

Has someone taken advantage of you?

Take heart; Jesus understands our predicaments. He will see to it, as He did in Tamar's case, that His laws will be honored because *He* does not lie to us at all. He is the Truth. Our Dayspring. Our Bright and Morning Star. King of kings. Lord of lords. He will not desert us in our time of need. I'm thankful that Tamar is in the genealogy of Christ. I'm glad to know that I have a fellow shame-sister out there, Tamar, who has tried to fix things herself and watched in shock as it all fell apart. I need real examples with real people and real solutions. I need a reality-based faith and Tamar's life helps to provide that for me. How about you?

My Prayer

Dear Lord, how much I am like Tamar. I confess I take matters into my own hands while you have a tapestry being sewn just for me. Help me to trust in You and Your Word as I face shame and loss—of a loved one, a divorce, depression, and many other things. Give me the strength to be patient and wait on your timing, which is perfect. Your Word is good: *"God is not a man, that he should lie, nor a son of man, that he should change his mind. Does he speak and then not act? Does he promise and not fulfill?"* (Numbers 23:19).

Give ear to my words, O Lord, consider my sighing. Listen to my cry for help, my King and my God, for to you I pray. In the morning I lay my requests before you and wait in expectation.
—Psalm 5:1–3

Your Prayer

From Pauper to Princess
Ruth

"Where you go I will go, and where you stay I will stay. Your people will be my people, and your God my God."
—Ruth 1:16*a*

Sin abounds and no one seems to escape family dysfunction. Ruth had no foreseeable future. She had no husband. She had no children. She had no obvious income. All she immediately possessed was a mother-in-law who went from pleasant to bitter in a short span of time due to various misfortune. All of a sudden, Ruth, a Moabite woman, had a key decision to make—leave Naomi, her Israelite mother-in-law, or do what her name meant in Hebrew. *Ruth,* may carry overtones of "friendship or closely associated with." She could be closely associated with—best friend—with her mother-in-law Naomi, whose name means "pleasant," but who quickly turned into what her new name, Mara, means: bitter.

However, Ruth's destiny was more than she could foresee; God planned for her to be the second woman named in the genealogy of Christ.

WEEK 3 • DAY 1
A FIRST STEP

"One thing I do know. I was blind but now I see."
—John 9:25*b*

Ruth, a Gentile widow, followed her heart and, in conjunction with her widowed mother-in-law, Naomi, went with Naomi back to a country, people, and God Ruth did not know.

Every woman who has felt shame in her life, regardless of how that shame manifests, longs to see a pauper such as Ruth turned into a princess. Because women who have known shame feel so much of the time like ugly ducklings, we leap and cheer silently in our hearts when a fellow sister is kissed by the prince (literally by Boaz and figuratively by Jesus).

In the days when the judges ruled, there was a famine in the land, and a man from Bethlehem in Judah, together with his wife and two sons, went to live for a while in the country of Moab. The man's name was Elimelech, his wife's name was Naomi, and the names of his two sons were Mahlon and Kilion. They were Ephrathites from Bethlehem, Judah. And they went to Moab and lived there.

Now Elimelech, Naomi's husband, died, and she was left with her two sons. They married Moabite women, one named Orpah and the other Ruth. After they had lived there about ten years, both Mahlon and Kilion also died, and Naomi was left without her two sons and her husband.
—Ruth 1:1–5

Naomi's worst nightmare had become a reality. She had not only lost her husband but also her two sons to death. Now, all she had were two Moabite daughters-in-law and herself to feed.

What kind of feelings do you think Naomi had at this point in her life?

We have all lost loved ones. Express your feelings about your loss:

I wrote about my experience and I believe I know how Naomi felt and why she wanted to be called *Mara*.

SOMEWHERE

Somewhere along the path I lost my
way.
Somewhere along the way I lost my
hope.
Somehow without my hope I found
resentment.
Somehow my resentment turned to
anger.
Somehow my anger grew into
bitterness.
Somehow my bitterness flew into rage.
Somehow my rage consumed me.

Somewhere in the rage I blamed You,
O God.
For all the pain.
For all the abandonment.
For all the fear.
For all the injustices.
For all the loneliness.
For all the sorrow.
For all the grief.
For all the tears.
For all the dreams never lived.
For all the hopes left unfulfilled.

Do you know, O God, how difficult
this is for me?
To take your hand and trust You—
in what I cannot see.

You know my past and pain so well,
for it is real to me.
Can You take my tattered life
and help me live for eternity?

Somewhere along the road, O Lord,
I gave my heart.

Somewhere along the trodden path
I lost those that I loved.

If I give to You my honesty
and choose to do what is right,
will You in turn give me the strength
to last the good and holy fight?

Because I come before You as a little
child
So very, very lost.
Somewhere along the way I blamed
You
for all my pain and thus the cost.

—*Deb Vanderslice*

God's Word explains the crossroads at which Ruth found herself with Naomi, and how Ruth found Him.

When she heard in Moab that the LORD had come to the aid of his people by providing food for them, Naomi and her daughters-in-law prepared to return home from there. With her two daughters-in-law she left the place where she had been living and set out on the road that would take them back to the land of Judah. Then Naomi said to her two daughters-in-law, "Go back, each of you, to your mother's home. May the LORD show kindness to you, as you have shown to your dead and to me. May the LORD grant that each of you will find rest in the home of another husband."

Then she kissed them and they wept aloud and said to her, "We will go back with you to your people."

But Naomi said, "Return home, my daughters. Why would you come with me? Am I going to have any more sons, who could become your husbands? Return home, my daughters; I am too old to have another husband. Even if I thought there was still hope for me—even if I had a husband tonight and then gave birth to sons—would you wait until they grew up? Would you remain unmarried for them? No, my daughters. It is more bitter for me than for you, because the LORD's hand has gone out against me!"

At this they wept again. Then Orpah kissed her mother-in-law good-by, but Ruth clung to her.

"Look," said Naomi, "your sister-in-law is going back to her people and her gods. Go back with her."

But Ruth replied, "Don't urge me to leave you or to turn back from you. Where you go I will go, and where you stay I will stay. Your people will be my people and your God my God. Where you die I will die, and there I will be buried. May the LORD deal with me, be it ever so severely, if anything but death separates you and me."
—Ruth 1:6–17

Ruth decided to trust in God.

How do we know that Naomi must have had an impact on Ruth? Be specific:

So the two women went on until they came to Bethlehem. When they arrived in Bethlehem, the whole town was stirred because of them, and the women exclaimed "Can this be Naomi." Don't call me Naomi," she told them. "Call me Mara because the Almighty has made my life very bitter. I went away full, but the LORD has brought me back empty. Why call me Naomi? The LORD has afflicted me, the Almighty has brought misfortune upon me.
—Ruth 1:19–22

What do you think was the reason the entire city came out to view Naomi?

What or whom does Naomi blame?

How does Naomi describe herself?

What does Naomi want to be called? Why?

Have you ever felt empty in your walk due to a loss or for another reason?

Losing a loved one can have a decisive and difficult impact on surviving family and friends. When my friend Martha died at age 30, I felt as though the world went on but that I remained in slow motion. I wrote this after she died. See if you can relate if you have lost a loved one.

THE REFINING

Sometimes this grief washes over me
like the ocean waves crashing against the sand.
Unending. Ceaseless. Perpetual.
To the mere spectator turned vacationer
the water brings with it peace, solitude, and rest.
But to the resident who beaches upon
its shore day after day and month after month,
the waves carry pain, loneliness, and grief.
How long, O Lord,
Will the waters captivate my life?
My every move. Thought. Response.
My world stopped while the world rudely went on.
My tears flowed unceasingly while others seemed to smile effortlessly.
Where is my hope, O God?
Who is my avenger today, O Lord?
Why do these lips honestly confess the horrors of my heart?
For whatever is gone now
I can rest assured that
You are still in control,
and will one day reveal the seemingly painful madness
of the here and now,
to the overwhelmingly speechless perfection
of Your divine plan.
Your method is perfect.
Your timing is perfect.
Your refining is perfect.
May this life of mine not tarry in vain
as I seek Your hand during this molding process.

—Deb Vanderslice

God's Word can bring us great comfort in the midst of death and the difficult circumstances that surround it and other losses.

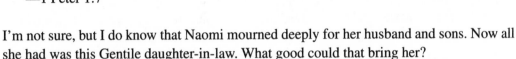

> *These have come so that your faith—of greater worth than gold, which perishes even though refined by fire—may be proved genuine and may result in praise, glory and honor when Jesus Christ is revealed.*
> —1 Peter 1:7

I'm not sure, but I do know that Naomi mourned deeply for her husband and sons. Now all she had was this Gentile daughter-in-law. What good could that bring her?

The story could have ended there if Ruth hadn't been so persistent. Naomi wanted to return to her home area of Bethlehem to grieve and put back the broken pieces of her life. Naomi's other daughter-in-law, Orpah, said goodbye to Naomi, but "Ruth clung to her [Naomi]" (Ruth 1:14*b*). It is interesting to note that the word *clung* appears here. Ruth's devotion to her mother-in-law is certainly admirable. This may remind us of when Mary Magdalene clung to Jesus at the Resurrection.

Why do you think Ruth went with Naomi to a foreign land, people, and God?

Do you think Ruth might have felt abandoned? Have you ever felt this way?

What type of shame was associated with Ruth's, Orpah's, and Naomi's widowhood?

What should be and what is the impact of an intimate relationship with God on feelings of abandonment and loss?

WEEK 3 • DAY 2
A POSITIVE CONFESSION

"Where you go I will go and where you stay I will stay. Your people will be my people and your God my God."
—Ruth 1:16

There it is—Ruth's confession to follow the God of the Israelites. This Gentile widow follows her heart and traveled back to Jerusalem, in conjunction with her widowed mother-in-law. All Ruth knew was that she had to follow Naomi. Again, as with the other women listed in the genealogy of Christ, it was a seemingly desperate act by a shamed woman.

With her confession of God fresh on her mind, Ruth accompanies Naomi back to where Naomi was well known.

In what ways do you think Ruth felt shame in this new environment?

Ruth was not an Israelite. She did not know the customs of the place. She didn't know anyone—not one soul except for Naomi. Perhaps that is why she clung to her mother-in-law. Or maybe she clung to her because of her heart. It takes a special person to move in with her mother-in-law, don't you think? Like Naomi, Ruth arrived in Bethlehem broken and bruised, without a husband or children. The shame must have multiplied with every word of gossip going on in Bethlehem.

Do you think Ruth's shame was different than Naomi's shame? Why?

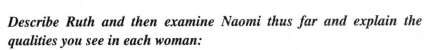

To what kind of work did Ruth and Naomi resort? They were both without means to survive. Ruth came up with an answer. *"And Ruth, the Moabitess said to Naomi, 'Let me go to the fields and pick up the leftover grain behind anyone in whose eyes I find favor'"* (Ruth 2:23).

Describe Ruth and then examine Naomi thus far and explain the qualities you see in each woman:

Even though Ruth had such wonderful qualities as a human being, she endured shame as a result of her Moabite culture, working in the fields, and having no children or husband. She endured the scorn of the nay-sayers in town. But notice this very small detail: Her future husband saw her hard work and that would eventually lead to their courtship.

Are there any jobs that you would be embarrassed to have?

How humble does God desire us to be? Enough that we better be nice to the pickup-window workers at the drive-through at the fast-food restaurants.

Yet another of Ruth's qualities were her humility and her diligence. This hardworking woman was noticed by a relative of Naomi's husband's clan. The relative's name? Boaz. Boaz noticed Ruth's hard work and tells her what to do.

> So Boaz said to Ruth, "My daughter, listen to me. Don't go and glean in another field and don't go away from here. Stay here with my servant girls. Watch the field where the men are harvesting, and follow along after the girls. I have told the men not to touch you. And whenever you are thirsty, go and get a drink from the water jars the men have filled."
> —Ruth 2:8–12

Ruth then asks Boaz a question I ask all the time. *"Why have I found such favor in your eyes that you notice me, a foreigner?"* (Ruth 2:10). Maybe you don't ever pose that question to God, but I ask Him why He is so good to me. Boaz tells Ruth:

> *"I've been told all about what you have done for your mother-in-law since the death of your husband—how you left your father and mother and her homeland and came to live with a people you did not know before. May the LORD repay you for what you have done. May you be richly rewarded by the LORD, the God of Israel, under whose wings you have come to take refuge.*
> —Ruth 2:11–12

Boaz tells Ruth she will be rewarded for her faith, a faith she really knows little about.

> *So Ruth stayed close to the servant girls of Boaz to glean until the barley and wheat harvests were finished. And she lived with her mother-in-law.*
> —Ruth 2:23

The Scripture states that Ruth stayed close to the servant girls of Boaz according to the instructions from her mother-in-law's kinsman. Ruth stayed close to her *kinsman-redeemer*. Ruth had found out that her only hope was Boaz.

Why is this mentioned? In that culture, a near-relative (or "kinsman") had certain privileges so he might step in and champion the cause of one who needed help (as a "redeemer"). A kinsman-redeemer was a *go'el*, which meant to redeem or buy back. In the Old Testament, it was law for any poor person to sell himself or herself into slavery, due to debt. It was up to his or her nearest relative to step in and buy back that person or property.

In what ways do you stay close to and are you dependent on Christ?

WEEK 3 • DAY 3
A CLOSER WALK

Spread the corner of your garment over me, since you are a kinsman redeemer."
—Ruth 3:9

It is important to note here that Naomi directs her daughter-in-law Ruth to go to Boaz's home turf and when he is finally asleep, to uncover his feet and lie down at his feet.

Ruth's actions were designed to provoke marriage. The act of uncovering Boaz's feet and lying down was a customary way to ask for marriage.

Ruth approached quietly uncovered his feet and lay down. In the middle of the night something startled the man, and he turned and discovered a woman lying at his feet. "Who are you?" he asked. "I am your servant Ruth," she said. "Spread the corner of your garment over me, since you are a kinsman redeemer."
—Ruth 3:7b–9

This image reminds me of the fact that all of us are able to come to the feet of the Cross, regardless of our past shame.

Should we not go to Christ sincerely and humbly, as Ruth did to Boaz?

Ruth said to Boaz, *"I am your servant Ruth."*

Having a woman in your bedroom late at night might give residents room to gossip or talk poorly about the woman.

Before you talk the next time at the water cooler, take a minute and ask yourself if the talk is upright and true or is just being said for mere entertainment.

Look up Ruth 3:10–17. Why did Boaz give some barley to Ruth?

Christ, like Boaz, is concerned with every detail of our lives, including our reputations. As we see in God's Word, we are not to gossip about others and destroy their reputation.

- Proverbs 11:13
- Proverbs 16:28
- Proverbs 26:22

I bet that at some point of her journey, Ruth, thought, *What have I gotten myself into?* I think that she probably felt emptiness too.

What fear might Ruth have had about being vulnerable?

What does God want us to lay at the foot of the Cross so that He can cover it?

Our tears, fears, sin, and shame are why Jesus came—not merely to shout from heaven above and say, "I understand," but rather to whisper down below on earth and say, "I know; your shame is My glory."

There's just one rule. We must give Him everything. This includes our brokenness and pain. Perhaps this is the most difficult.

What is your pain? A divorce? A death? An unfair and sadistic act where you got no vote at all at how the hand played out? Was it a rape by someone you knew? Perhaps the scars were physical? Maybe the marks were left unseen by others but known blindly by you. Was it an illness that wouldn't or doesn't go away? A broken relationship that refuses to heal and only gets worse each year? The list could go on and on.

Abuses and sins are never kept to themselves. Maybe,

because of the sin done to you, you now imprison yourself with guilt, shame, and unforgiveness and refuse to let go. Perhaps you've taken the place of your captor who has long been gone. A prison of pain is a funny thing. Sometimes we say we want to be free, and yet we are the judge, jury, and executioner of our own mandated sentences.

Does He who knows us inside-and-out not know this? Take a chance, please. I did. I finally let myself off the hook. I took responsibility for the ways in which I had responded to the sin done to me and decided to let go of the hatred, anger, and rage. Was it scary? Let's just say it hasn't been dull. Every insecurity of mine was thrust front and center. Instead of shame reigning supreme, peace eventually ruled my life. I won't lie and say that my doors of prison have instantly flown open. Not true.

However, each time I get real by being honest with God, the real me steps forward and begs for my Abba, my heavenly Father to take me into His arms and comfort me. For it is not because of me I am accepted, but because of what He alone did for me. He took my shame and bore it that fateful Friday on the Cross.

Does God truly fathom the ways in which we have been shamed and the pain we carry?

Oh yes, He knows all too well. Remember, He was crucified for being God. For being perfect. A friend gave Him over for 30 pieces of silver. Another friend three times denied knowing Him. The rest of His friends fled when He faced His darkest hours. He was beaten beyond recognition. His clothes were taken away. He was murdered. He was God, remember? God in human form. He came to know our pain and shame and to give us hope.

He came to whisper to us on our bed of pain and in our longings that He truly understands. We can let Him be our Comforter and Redeemer today.

Do you know God as your Comforter and Redeemer? How do you know Him personally?

WEEK 3 • DAY 4
THE ULTIMATE RELATIVE

However, Boaz replied, "Although it is true that I am near of kin, there is a kinsman-redeemer nearer than I."
—Ruth 3:12

What did Boaz mean by this statement?

Though he was speaking of the natural, a relative closer to Ruth than Boaz, my own thoughts remind me that there is still One closer to Ruth than anyone else, though she did not realize this.

Meanwhile Boaz went up to the town gate and sat there. When the kinsman redeemer he had mentioned came along, Boaz said, "Come over here, my friend and sit down" So he went over and sat down. Boaz took ten of the elders of the town and said, "Sit here," and they did so. Then he said to the kinsman-redeemer, "Naomi, who has come back from Moab, is selling the piece of land that belonged to our brother Elimelech. I thought I should bring the matter to your attention and suggest that you buy it in the presence of these seated here and in the presence of the elders of my people. If you will redeem it, do so. But if you will not, tell me, so I will know. For no one has the right to do it except you, and I am next in line."'

"I will redeem it," he said.

Then Boaz said, "On the day you buy the land from Naomi and from Ruth the Moabitess, you acquire the dead man's widow, in order to maintain the name of the dead with his property."

At this the kinsman-redeemer said, "Then I cannot redeem it because I might endanger my own estate. You redeem it yourself. I cannot do that."

(Now in earlier times in Israel, for the redemption and transfer of property to become final, one party took off his sandal and gave it to the other. This was the method of legalizing transactions in Israel.)

So the kinsman-redeemer said to Boaz, "Buy it yourself." And he removed his sandal.
—Ruth 4:1–9

It is interesting to note that Boaz went up to the *"town gate and sat there"* (Ruth 4:1). Elders met at the city gate area, so that is why Boaz needed to go there to transact this business. (See Proverbs 31:23.) Thus, many witnesses would be present to hear and proceed with Boaz's predicament.

It probably wasn't much of a shock but the nearest relative happened to stop the transaction when the "baggage" came along with the deal...meaning Ruth. She was an outsider once again. It would be enormously generous of Boaz to redeem not only Naomi and her land, but also a Moabite.

In Old Testament times, a sandal was one sign of a transaction, much like our signature on a check. One man would take off his sandal in response to a deal and hand over his sandal as an acquisition or bill of sale. Did you notice what Ruth did during the entire deal-making process? Absolutely nothing. Not a thing. Notice that Ruth could not redeem herself. It had to be through the kinsman-redeemer that Ruth would be redeemed. Boaz and Ruth eventually married.

This love story of Ruth's is a picture of God's love story with us. Our salvation, our redemption is not achieved in any way by us, but rather by Jesus Christ. We play no purchase part in the entire process. It was up to God alone to provide our purchase price by His shed blood. It is up to God to call us to Himself and He woos us by His Spirit.

Many times, this creates a problem for some Christians when we witness to others about Christ's love. Instead of relying on the Holy Spirit to convict a person, many times we wrongly think we have presented a good gospel message and that salvation comes out of our own evangelizing heroics. Nothing could be farther from the truth. Boaz alone redeemed Ruth. God alone redeems.

Read and record your impressions of Psalm 49:7:

The word *full* is mentioned in this verse. Could it be that God desires for all of us to be *fully* redeemed?

What other "fully" things does God care about to give to us?

Make a list of specific ways you have been redeemed by Jesus Christ:

Although Ruth experienced shame due to her poverty, she had faith in Boaz, her kinsman-redeemer. Ruth, a Moabite, is a perfect example of how it is not bloodline and birth that determine one's faith, but rather it is our Kinsman-Redeemer and our relationship to Him. Ruth, a Gentile, steps out in courage to enter a new country, with new surroundings, and a new God to control her life.

Ruth is yet another example of how God's hand chooses to graft us into relationship with Jesus. Not only did Ruth overcome poverty, being a widow, and being an alien in a strange land. God also redeemed Naomi's emptiness and gave her fullness.

A son, Obed, was born to Ruth and Boaz and become the father of Jesse, King David's father, and an ancestor of Christ.

Thus, God used bad circumstances, such as the case of Naomi's husband and two sons' deaths, and brought forth good from it all. Ruth and Boaz's son, Obed, is a surrogate son to Naomi. She is no longer bitter and empty, but rather has become pleasant and full.

So Boaz took Ruth and she became his wife. Then he went to her, and the LORD enabled her to conceive, and she gave birth to a son. The women said to Naomi, "Praise be to the LORD, who this day has not left you without a kinsman redeemer. May he become famous throughout Israel! He will renew your life and sustain you in your old age. For your daughter-in-law, who loves you and who is better to you than seven sons, has given him birth."

Then Naomi took the child, laid him in her lap and cared for him. The women living there said, "Naomi has a son." And they named him Obed. He was the father of Jesse, the father of David.

This, then, is the family line of Perez: Perez was the father of Hezron, Hezron the father of Ram, Ram the father of Amminadab, Amminadab the father of Nahshon, Nahshon the father of Salmon, Salmon the father of Boaz, Boaz the father of Obed, Obed the father of Jesse, and Jesse the father of David.
—Ruth 4:13–22

Ruth went from being a pauper to a princess, so to speak. God took a desolate and poverty stricken Gentile, an outsider, whom He placed in the lineage of Tamar and her son Perez, by giving her a kinsman-redeemer in Tamar's descendant Boaz. God ordained, God chose, and God established this outsider, Ruth, and made her grandmother to King David.

Ruth's confession to God made her an insider. Her willingness to be humble before God, to step out in faith towards Him, and to go to a foreign land were part of God's plan for His glory. He led her to become the second woman listed in the genealogy of Christ.

Every woman who has felt shame in her life, regardless of how that shame incorporated itself, longs to see a pauper, such as Ruth, turned into a princess.

Because we as women have known shame and feel so much of the time like ugly ducklings, we can cheer silently in our hearts when a fellow shame-sister is kissed by the prince, (Boaz literally and Christ figuratively) and finally becomes a princess.

We can be encouraged today. There is One near who longs to be our Kinsman-Redeemer.

Is Jesus your Kinsman-Redeemer?

Many modern fairy tales are reminiscent of Ruth's story. However, Ruth's life and God's redemptive power is not a fable. These are fact available through God's Holy Word.

And like Naomi, we can either be empty or full. Like Ruth, we can choose to follow a merciful God by coming into relationship with Him through His Son. I don't know about you, but I'm going to try to stay close to my Kinsman-Redeemer and pick up the morsels He leaves behind just for me.

Week 3 • Day 5
The Illumination

"I will lead the blind by ways they have not known, I will turn the darkness into light before them and make the rough places smooth."
—Isaiah 42:16

Even with God's redemption, we will all have struggle in this life. We know that Ruth saw many dark days until she met Boaz, her kinsman-redeemer. Yet Ruth became a great woman whom God used to give Himself glory. Here, a woman of no status found favor in her blind walk of faith with her mother-in-law.

How would you have reacted had you been in the same position as Ruth?

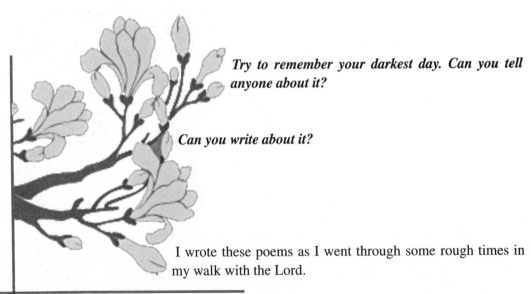

Try to remember your darkest day. Can you tell anyone about it?

Can you write about it?

I wrote these poems as I went through some rough times in my walk with the Lord.

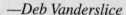

I'm venturing down a road, O Lord
that doesn't feel quite familiar.
I'm unsure where it's leading
yet that stops me not.
It is a dangerous steep path
and nothing is comfortable, O dear God.
I find myself unable to go back
where predictability was my refuge.
Something is beckoning me further on this road,
so addicting in its uncertainty.
Could it be, O sweet Jesus
that what draws me towards the darkness
is the illumination of You?
For in this blind walk of mine perhaps
I'm finally beginning to see who You are and whose I really am.

—*Deb Vanderslice*

BED OF PAIN

"My tears have been my food day and night."
—Isaiah 42:3

Lay down upon this bed of pain.
The sorrows deep you can't contain.
I come gently to tuck you in
and hold you close from evil's den.
Though your hurt is a well dug deep
I'll soften your pillow so you will sleep.
The bliss of peace will overflow
My healing love you will know.
Sleep well with this longing of Mine.
For I'm the Bliss you will find.

—*Deb Vanderslice*

Can you also write about your Kinsman-Redeemer experience?

God has whispered to us that He knows what our "bed of pain" is all about. We can have many sorrows and difficulties in our lives. Mine happened to be the grief of losing a close friend, my ongoing struggle with depression, and a divorce. Like Isaiah says, tears were my food at all times of the day and night.

Does God fathom our pains? Even the smallest concerns?

What is one detail in your life or in a loved one's life that is bothering you?

God cares about all the details. *"All my longings lie open before you O Lord"* (Psalm 38:9). Even our hearts' whispers to the Lord. I know a woman who said that she has seen God answer even the least desire of her heart, before—and whether or not—she prays.

If we can't pray for the smallest of needs, then why pray for the greatest of needs? Do you know what? I once prayed for a parking space during the Christmas rush one day. And lo and behold, I got it!

What would happen if we only did what Paul told us to do: *"Do not be anxious about anything (football or parking*

94

spaces), *but in everything, by prayer and petition, with thanksgiving, present your requests to God"* (Philippians 4:6). I challenge you to pray for one week about the details of your life. You can record the request and then pray each day for an answer of yes, no, or wait. I can't tell you how much this has transformed my prayer life.

Are you willing to pray unceasingly, with thanksgiving, for an answer?

Now make a list of all the details you have in your life that you are worrying about. Record them so you can see the hand of God moving as He answers your requests for... even a parking space:

For God, who said, "Let light shine out of darkness.
—Genesis 1:3

Made his light shine in our hearts to give us the light of the knowledge of the glory of God in the face of Christ.
—2 Corinthians 4:6

My Prayer

Dear Lord, thank You that we can be grafted into the tree of life with You. Let us be committed to You as Ruth was—totally abandoned to You alone. Forgive us when we falter along the way. Help us to stay focused on You, our Kinsman-Redeemer and to stay close to You at Your feet. Give us strength to fight the good fight of faith, in spite of Satan, and even those around us who try to discourage us. Let us remember that we trust You with what cannot be seen. Amen.

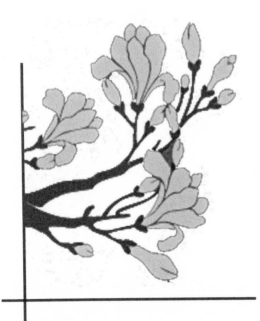

Your Prayer

A Talked-About Woman

Bathsheba

One evening David got up from his bed and walked around on the roof of the palace. From the roof he saw a woman bathing. The woman was very beautiful, and David sent someone to find out about her. The man said, "Isn't this Bathsheba, the daughter of Eliam and the wife of Uriah the Hittite?" Then David sent messengers to get her. She came to him, and he slept with her. (She had purified herself from her uncleanness.) Then she went back home. The woman conceived and sent word to David saying, "I am pregnant."
—2 Samuel 11:2–5

Adultery. Pregnancy out-of-wedlock. Complicity in the murder of a spouse. Marriage to the murderer, who is the king. Death of the illegitimate infant son. A second pregnancy. Birth of another son and then more children.

Although mistakes plague everyone, not everyone's sins are visible for all to see . . . except if you've made those errors with the man in charge of a nation.

This all sounds like a soap opera, doesn't it? A beautiful woman bathing herself. Her her husband is away at war on behalf of the kingdom. The handsome king is not on the front lines with his troops. He is overlooking his balcony this night, watching one of his soldier's wife bathing.

But it's not a soap opera. It is the true story of events involving Bathsheba. I believe that one reason this particular biblical story from the Old Testament was recorded is so that we can to learn some valuable lessons. First of all, sin does not happen overnight. Sin likes to hang around, lurking, day in and day out, trying to snag a customer or two.

Sin is no laughing matter. It lurks on the street corner like an appealing wayward woman, hoping to snag a customer or two who ventures her way. Make no doubt about it, Satan will muster all his strength to catch a patron.

Then out came a woman to meet him,
dressed like a prostitute and with crafty intent.
(She is loud and defiant,
her feet never stay at home;
now in the street, now in the squares,
at every corner she lurks.)
She took hold of him and kissed him
and with a brazen face she said:
"I have fellowship offerings at home;
today I fulfilled my vows.
So I came out to meet you;
I looked for you and have found you!
I have covered my bed
with colored linens from Egypt.
I have perfumed my bed
with myrrh, aloes and cinnamon.
Come, let's drink deep of love till morning;
let's enjoy ourselves with love!
My husband is not at home;
he has gone on a long journey.
He took his purse filled with money
and will not be home till full moon."
With persuasive words she led him astray;
she seduced him with her smooth talk.
All at once he followed her
like an ox going to the slaughter,
like a deer stepping into a noose
till an arrow pierces his liver,
like a bird darting into a snare,
little knowing it will cost him his life.
—Proverbs 7

WEEK 4 • DAY 1
THE LOCATION OF SIN

In the spring, at the time when kings go off to war . . . David
remained in Jerusalem.
—2 Samuel 11:1

The whole affair could have been averted if David would have been
in the right and proper location at the time. But he wasn't. Scripture does not tell us
specifically the reason why David was not with his troops in battle, though one of his
commanders had encouraged David to remain in the palace as his fighting men went off to
battle. All we know is that David remained in Jerusalem. That seems to be the location of
sin. Disobedience has a price and David will be one of the participants who pays.

Read the following verses on sin and record your overall impression below:

"If you do what is right, will you not be accepted? But if you do not do what is right,
sin is crouching at your door; it desires to have you, but you must master it."
—Genesis 4:7

"But if you fail to do this, you will be sinning against the Lord; and you may be
sure that your sin will find you out."
—Numbers 32:23b

For in his own eyes he flatters himself too much to detect or hate his sin.
—Psalm 36:2

"Thanks be to God—through Jesus Christ our Lord! So then, I myself in my mind
am a slave to God's law, but in the sinful nature a slave to the law of sin."
—Romans 7:25

Then, after desire has conceived, it gives birth to sin; and sin, when it is full-grown,
gives birth to death.
—James 1:15

Satan assembles all his repertoire and persuades David, the king, to remain at home while his troops go into battle. The location of David's sin is his home. If David had been more responsible in his kingly responsibility, and been off at war during the spring, he would not have ventured out on his roof that fateful spring evening.

Sometimes I think we view Satan as a red-dressed horned creature who only occupies the pits of hell. However, he is much craftier than that. Subtle and persistent.

Look up the following verses on Satan:

And no wonder, for Satan himself masquerades as an angel of light.
—2 Corinthians 11:14

One day the angels came to present themselves before the Lord, and Satan also came with them. The Lord said to Satan, "Where have you come from?" Satan answered the Lord, "From roaming through the earth and going back and forth in it."
—Job 1:6–7

"The thief comes only to steal and kill and destroy."
—John 10:10

Name a time when you were lured into sin over a slow period of time:

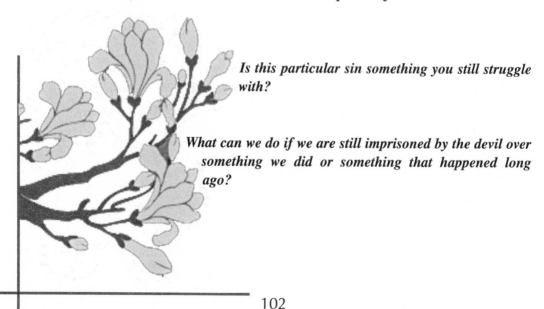

Is this particular sin something you still struggle with?

What can we do if we are still imprisoned by the devil over something we did or something that happened long ago?

WEEK 4 • DAY 2
THE LUST OF SIN

One evening David got up from his bed and walked around on the roof of the palace...From the roof he saw a woman bathing. The woman was very beautiful, and David sent someone to find out about her.
—2 Samuel 11:2–3a

Next there is the lust of sin. David *sees* someone desirable and decides he must have her. After all, he *is* the king. *"Then David sent messengers to get her. She came to him, and he slept with her"* (2 Samuel 11:4). Look closely at Bathsheba's dilemma. She was married and yet the king of Israel requested that she come see him. If Bathsheba declined, she might have suffered severe consequence, even death. Either way, she was trapped. Don't go—and suffer the king's wrath, or go and commit adultery.

When was the last time you faced a serious predicament?

Record what 2 Samuel 11:3b states:

David clearly found out that Bathsheba was a married woman. It is worth noting that her husband Uriah's name indicates that even though he was a Hittite, he had probably adopted the Israeli's faith because the name *Uriah* in Hebrew means, "The Lord is light."

Why is this important to know?

What actions of obedience do you see throughout this story that shows us that Uriah was devoted to the Israeli faith or morality?

Then David sent messengers to get her. She came to him, and he slept with her. (She had purified herself from her uncleanness.) Then she went back home. The woman conceived and sent word to David, saying, "I am pregnant."
—2 Samuel 11:4–5

David not only saw Bathsheba and lusted after her, but he also sent more than one messenger. Why would God put this in His perfect Word? Why the plurality of messengers? I believe it is to show us that David was a powerful and influential king. Just imagine being a woman and having more than one of the king's messengers knock at your door. Dare you refuse to go with them to the king?

It was customary that if the king of Israel beckoned you, you went, or else faced his punishment. So, Bathsheba went.

What do you think was going through Bathsheba's mind at this point?

She went to him, and he slept with her. Then she went back home. Then she became pregnant and sent word to David.

Through his actions, David is guilty of breaking the sixth, seventh, ninth, and tenth commandments. Look up Exodus 20:13–17 and record your impressions here:

If you are thinking that David alone was able, willing, and responsible since he had all the power, let us dig a little deeper into God's Word. God makes note that Bathsheba had purified herself first. Why this verse, do you think? She appears to have been a willing participant because she cleansed herself, indicating her condition at the time of her sexual intercourse with David. She had become ceremonially clean after the seven-day period of monthly impurity due to having her period. This is extremely important because it shows us she is pregnant by David and not by her husband who is off on the battlefield.

Look up Leviticus 15:19–30 and record your impressions:

*Record Proverbs 31:30**a**:*

Because of location of David's sin—on his flat rooftop in springtime—shame rears its ugly head and lives are about to be destroyed.

What is your shame about? Was it something you did yourself or that someone did to you?

In what ways have you responded to that shame?

WEEK 4 • DAY 3
THE LANGUAGE OF SIN

"The heart is deceitful above all things."
—Jeremiah 17:9

Record your impressions of these verses:
Leviticus 20:10

Deuteronomy 22:22

According to God's Word, what should have happened to David and Bathsheba?

They should have been killed—executed. But they weren't. God had mercy on them. Read what God does when we are caught in the act of sin and escape unscathed: *"The Lord our God is merciful and forgiving, even though we have rebelled against him"* (Daniel 9:9).

Even though we understand that David exercised his power as a king to engage in sin, and that he committed adultery but what about Bathsheba's actions? This woman purposely cleansed herself, so that there would be no question that her husband was not the father of her baby. Deceitfulness. Cunning. Deception. Duplicity. Dishonesty. Betrayal. Bathsheba thought it.

After Bathsheba told David she was pregnant by him, David again abused his authority and power to deceive Bathsheba's husband, Uriah. David's plan, first, was to call Uriah home from war and then have him sleep with his wife, thus making Uriah think he was the father of the baby.

Then David said to Uriah, "Go down to your house and wash your feet." So Uriah left the palace...But Uriah slept at the entrance to the palace with all his master's servants and did not go down to his house."
—2 Samuel 11:8

Uriah, a man of honor, chose to remain and to serve his master, David, rather than fulfill his own sexual desires with his wife, Bathsheba. Therefore, David resorted to another plan; to get Uriah drunk and send him staggering on his way to his wife and their bed.

Then David said to him, "Stay here one more day, and tomorrow I will send you back." So Uriah remained in Jerusalem that day and the next. At David's invitation, he ate and drank with him, and David made him drunk. But in the evening Uriah went out to sleep on his mat among his master's servants; he did not go home.
—2 Samuel 11:12–13

It was evident to King David at this point that Uriah was devoted to him and would not be returning to Bathsheba. So David, out of desperation, tried to cover up his adultery, and therefore shame, by having Uriah murdered.

In the morning David wrote a letter to Joab and sent it with Uriah. In it he wrote, "Put Uriah in the front line where the fighting is fiercest. Then withdraw from him so he will be struck down and die."
—2 Samuel 11:14

That is exactly what happened. David arranged Uriah's murder and Uriah unknowingly carried his own death orders to Joab.

See how King David went to great lengths to fool Bathsheba's husband, Uriah, that he, not David, had impregnated Bathsheba. In order to do this, what did David do?

In 2 Samuel 11:11, what does Uriah's response to David tell us about Uriah's character?

Is there any evidence of resistance on the part of Bathsheba to David's plans?

Do you recall a time when you were less than honest? Did you justify your deceit somehow?

Was there ever a time when you stood by and let someone else speak for you, knowing that the person speaking for you was being dishonest?

Do you think silence sometimes equals sin? When?

Is this what happened with Bathsheba?

At first glance, we may think it cruel that the baby born to David and Bathsheba was destined to die. But, after further examination, we can say with relative confidence that the child would die *"so that the work of God might be displayed"* (John 9:3).

David's enemies were outraged. According to Jewish law, David could have been put to death due to his adultery with Bathsheba, as well as the murder of Uriah. However, he escapes, as does Bathsheba, mercifully. This infuriates David's enemies. However, the child conceived in sin would not escape.

It was not until Nathan the prophet told King David a story that David finally confessed his sin before God and man. He called it what it was. No more dressing up the language of sin. Just look at the remorse of David.

"Have mercy on me, O God, according to your unfailing love; according to your great compassion blot out my transgressions. Wash away all my iniquity and cleanse me from my sin. For I know my transgressions, and my sin is always before me. Against you, you only, have I sinned and done what is evil in your sight, so that you are proved right when you speak and justified when you judge. Surely I was sinful at birth, sinful from the time my mother conceived me. Surely you desire truth in the inner parts, you teach me wisdom in the inmost place. Cleanse me with hyssop, and I will be clean; wash me, and I will be whiter than snow. Let me hear joy and gladness; let the bones you have crushed rejoice. Hide your face from my sins and blot out all my iniquity. Create in me a pure heart, O God, and renew a steadfast spirit within me."
—Psalm 51:1–10

Have you been remorseful and repentant toward your sin?

Most of us would admit that at a time or two, we have gone along with the crowd, gone along with sin.

WEEK 4 • DAY 4
BATHSHEBA'S DESPERATION

"Listen to my cry, for I am in desperate need; rescue me from those who pursue me, for they are too strong for me. Set me free from my prison."
Psalm 142:6–7a

I believe Bathsheba was curious. I know it's not found in Scripture, but I wonder if Bathsheba was inquisitive about the king and his palace. What would it have been like for her to visit King David in all his splendor? What would complete autonomy have felt like?

Which of us would fault Bathsheba for her willingness to submit to King David? However, as in all extramarital affairs, there may have been something left unfulfilled in her marriage to Uriah. Perhaps she felt undesirable even though others thought she was all right. Maybe she was inadequate in her own eyes. Whatever feelings Bathsheba acted on to engage in an affair, you can be sure of this: the revolving door of shame was there to keep her in the cycle of shame.

What's your shame over? A divorce? An abuse? A failure? An abortion? In what areas or addictions does this shame manifest itself? Eating disorders? Alcohol abuse? Drug abuse? Workaholism? Does silence rid us of our shame? No.

I've been there; I've traveled nowhere in that revolving door of shame. Satan is always in the midst of sin, but therein lies the overwhelming goodness of God's grace. God, seeing us in the throngs of sin and shame, uses that very same shame to turn it into His eternal glory.

Yes, Bathsheba cheated on her loyal husband without so much as a word. Yes, she willfully participated in a scheme to make her husband think he impregnated her instead of David. Yes, she waited in the wings while David murdered her husband in a very cowardly manner. Yes, she endured the birth of an illegitimate son. Yes, she experienced the death of that illegitimate son. Yes, she married King David. Yes, she was comforted at the birth of a second son. And yes, God redeemed Bathsheba's shame by allowing her to give birth and raise this second son...the wisest human (for awhile) to ever walk the planet, except for Christ.

Can't you just hear the hecklers by the Monday morning water cooler—in this case, by the well—drawing water for the thirsty camels?

"Hey, did you hear about Bathsheba? Yeah, she got pregnant by King David. I hear that Uriah's death wasn't an accident. Now she's going to marry the king. Doesn't matter though. The child will still be illegitimate in Israel's eyes."

And so the earthly story goes.

However, God in heaven has a completely different view. God takes a sinning *"man after his own heart"* (1 Samuel 13:14) and unites this David with a woman of shame to produce the wisest king ever to sit on the throne of Israel. Adultery? Yes. Deceit? Without a doubt. Lies? Of course. Murder? Definitely.

What made the God of the universe choose Bathsheba to be counted in the genealogy of Christ? Was it her faithfulness? No. Her heartfelt prayers? No. How about her honesty and truthfulness? None of the above. God took a woman, a married woman no less, and showed us this woman at her worst and turned her shame into His glory.

I once heard a pastor say that he did not want to be put up on a shelf or silenced for committing grave sins during his tenure or ministry. That is, he believed that God would silence him, much like a candle put away on a shelf and no longer of any service. I couldn't disagree more. After all, doesn't Isaiah 42:3 say, *"a smoldering wick he will not snuff out"*? Who is righteous enough to say who exactly God will use for His divine service? If Jesus's genealogy is any indicator, then the likes of prostitutes, adulteresses, and liars seem to be the norm and not the exception.

What about the commonality of God consistently choosing to go outside the perceived status quo of the Israelites to overwhelmingly choose defiled and scarred Gentiles to grace the lineage of the incarnate God Himself? Want more proof that God desires to rob Satan at his conception of shame? Well, just look at that thing we all view every day: the mirror. I did, and it flabbergasted me that, in spite of myself, He still allows me to open my mouth, or rather, pick up my pen, and raise my voice for His sake.

Why did God divinely place Bathsheba in the genealogy of Christ? Surely He could have chosen someone else. True. But He didn't. Maybe He wanted those of us in difficult circumstances, or no-win situations, to know that there is hope.

You see, friend, in the immediate situation Bathsheba came out a loser any way you look at it. One, she could have refused the king and died. Two, she could have slept with David and broken her marriage vows. Or three, she could have watched as David murdered her husband. Maybe you've been there too; somewhere between bad judgments and no help. There was no one advising Bathsheba. You might argue that she was a victim of circumstances. What about you? Did you suddenly, instantly find yourself caught up in an unanticipated event that you never asked for? Did you aimlessly stand by as your life spun out of control? Did you feel numb from lack of belief? Did your world go gray with doubt and fear? Did you get something in return for nothing?

Have you been in a similar situation lately?

Whether or not we have committed adultery, all of us who are born into original sin at conception. *"Surely I was sinful at birth, sinful from the time my mother conceived me"* (Psalm 51:5).

WEEK 4 • DAY 5
SHAME NO MORE

"No one whose hope is in you will ever be put to shame."
—Psalm 25:3*a*

God could have ended the story of David and Bathsheba after their firstborn son died. God was not obligated to do anything more for David and Bathsheba. He forgave them. Of course He restored them. And yes, He esteemed them. But what about their shame? The shame of not only adultery and murder, but now the death of their firstborn son as a result?

Why on earth did God take Bathsheba's firstborn? Wasn't the shame enough already? If we think the paparazzi in the pop culture today are bad, just think about what Bathsheba endured. She couldn't go anywhere without the constant finger-pointing and snickering and name calling. As for the marriage, word had more than likely leaked out that Uriah had been murdered. Their marriage, at best, was a cover-up. It didn't take a genius to figure out that David was the father of the baby. For nine agonizing months Bathsheba hid behind the palace doors. Behind her maids-in-waiting. The walls that once had beckoned her to a lover finally held her captive to the revolving door of shame. Day in, day out.

But then it happened. Grace appeared. Grace descended down like an early afternoon spring rain. Soothing. Soft. *"Then David comforted his wife Bathsheba, and he went to her and lay with her. She gave birth to a son, and they named him Solomon. The Lord loved him"* (2 Samuel 12:24).

Perhaps Bathsheba didn't know it, but she carried the wisest man (besides Jesus) in her womb. If her firstborn son would not have died, would David and she ever have had Solomon? Would her shame ever have been redeemed? Would God's glory have ever prevailed over the sin?

Let's not forget about *"And we know that in all things God works for the good of those who love him, who have been called according to his purpose"* (Romans 8:28). We will never know all the answers of this lifetime. Could it be that there is a divine purpose in everything? Can good actually come from bad, or more specifically, sorrow? Without a doubt, yes. We can see that the *"God of all comfort"*

(2 Corinthians 1:3) didn't merely forgive Bathsheba; He let her in on His glory. She would be part of the genealogy of Christ. Though David's Bathsheba experienced a lot of heartache, she also experienced grace.

So far, we have three sexually impure women and one desperate, codependent widow. It is as though God is proclaiming, "Come one come all, view the pristine, immaculate, perfect Lord of the universe, born from downtrodden and defiled women."

Read and record your impressions of what 1 Kings 3:7–14 says:

I've made blunders time and time again only to find myself clothed with shame. God desires to free us from our shame the same way He freed Bathsheba—by allowing Himself to enter our pain-ridden, heartbroken, tattered lives. No matter the sin, He pursues us, the sinners. Think you have to have it all together? Remember Tamar, Rahab, Ruth, and Bathsheba?

It is interesting to note that in the genealogy of Jesus, the Bible says, *"David was the father of Solomon, whose mother had been Uriah's wife"* (Matthew 1:6b). At first, it seems unbelievable. God uses David's credentials in full view, while He dismisses Bathsheba's name altogether. Shouldn't this be reversed? After all, David went one step further than Bathsheba. He murdered. But hold on for a second.

Bathsheba in Hebrew means "daughter of an oath." Thus, her name implies that she is bound to a truth of a promise to God Almighty. I don't think it is any accident that God eliminates Bathsheba's personal name in Matthew 1, while choosing instead to refer to her as the wife of Uriah. She mourned her husband's death a mere seven days before marrying King David.

Did Bathsheba really have any say in her adultery? She could have disobeyed and endured dire consequences or accommodate and live. Another theory as to why God refers to Bathsheba as "Uriah's wife" is that this had to do with her destiny or purpose.

What could we, as women, possibly learn from Bathsheba, the wife of Uriah? Well, unlike Tamar, who took things into her own hands, Bathsheba watched her life spin aimlessly out of control. Been there? Done that? I watched helplessly as everything I held dear slipped away in a split second.

Shame is ruthless. It likes to isolate, condemn, and humiliate until the life and light has gone out of you. So, while Bathsheba endured the shame of adultery and an out-of-wedlock pregnancy, God simply brought peace to her life through Solomon. Guess what *Solomon* means in Hebrew? That's right. It means "peace." Could it be that God redeemed Bathsheba's shame and replaced that very shame with His peace?

Maybe by telling us that Bathsheba was *"the mother of Solomon, who had been Uriah's wife,"* God wants us to remember that He honors both David and Uriah. David was, generally speaking, the faithful man *"after God's own heart"* (1 Samuel 13:14), while Uriah was the faithful man of a woman's heart, Bathsheba. Both David and Uriah played an honoring role in the life of Bathsheba.

Is your shame over sexual impurity? Did you go outside the bounds of marriage to find love and acceptance? Maybe you engaged in premarital sex. Did you have an out-of-wedlock pregnancy? Or perhaps you ended a pregnancy through an abortion. Think God is still holding it over you?

I suggest this: When Satan reminds you of your past, you remind him of his future; the lake of fire (Revelation 20:14–15).

Have you struggled for years, maybe decades with past sexual sins?

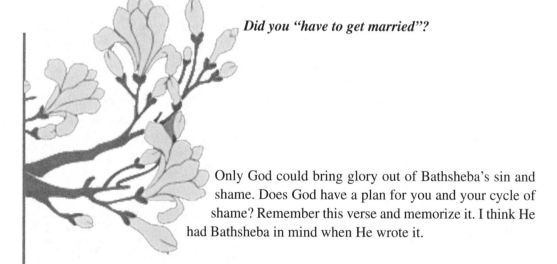

Did you "have to get married"?

Only God could bring glory out of Bathsheba's sin and shame. Does God have a plan for you and your cycle of shame? Remember this verse and memorize it. I think He had Bathsheba in mind when He wrote it.

"For I know the plans I have for you, declares the Lord, plans to prosper you and not to harm you, plans to give you a hope and a future."
—Jeremiah 29:11

Out of great shame can come great glory. I'd argue that God gave Bathsheba a double dose of peace. One, giving her Solomon, and two, listing her in the genealogy of Christ. Are we not in great company?

Do you ever feel unworthy and ashamed? What is it that makes you feel this way?

What does 1 John 1:9 say? Write it here:

Do you really believe God's Word? If so, why can you not forgive yourself?

What keeps us from living forgiven lives before God?

Look up in a Bible concordance God's Word concerning His forgiveness. Record a few verses and write your impressions of God's forgiveness to you and to all humanity:

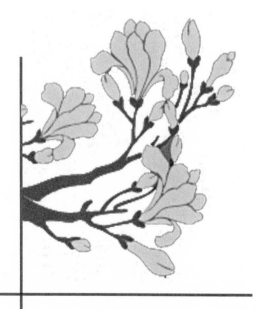

116

My Prayer

Dear Lord, help us to know our own personal locations of sin. Give us wisdom whenever we feel unworthy to serve You. Grant us the perseverance to fight off Satan's lies about our shame that manifests in different areas of our lives. Thank You for not giving up on us even when we do ourselves. In Jesus's name. Amen.

Your Prayer

Knock-Knock, God Calling

Rahab, and Mary, the Mother of Jesus

> *But God chose the foolish things of the world to shame the wise; God chose the*
> *weak things of the world to shame the strong.*
> —1 Corinthians 1:27

"Opportunity knocks," or so the saying goes. This week, we will study two more women God called out of shame to place in Jesus's genealogy. On days one and two, we will look at Rahab. The remainder of the week's study is devoted to Mary, Jesus's mother, the first of several women we will look at whose lives are recorded in the New Testament.

First, we'll examine how God used Rahab to extend grace to a couple of His followers. This prostitute (who also was know as an innkeeper), Rahab saw God's children literally knocking on her door, not only invites them in, but also hides, protects, and trusts them in obedience to her faith in God. A woman of the veil. A whore. Call her what you may, but God chose Rahab to be only one of the women in Jesus's genealogy. Surely there were others more qualified to fulfill that duty. Think about it. What if God chose to go down that dark alley in your city and pluck out your ancestor? That's exactly what God had in mind.

Week 5 • Day 1
A Day of Desperation

> *So they went and entered the house of a prostitute named Rahab and stayed there.*
> —Joshua 2:1

Are you beginning to see a pattern? God delights in taking sinful, impulse-ridden, and weak people to transform them into His pure, patient, and strong new creations. *"My grace is sufficient for you, for my power is made perfect in weakness"* (2 Corinthians 12:9a).

The Israelites had been in bondage and in the desert for 40 years. Moses has died and their new leader, Joshua, was leading the Israelite children into the Promised Land. Joshua sent out two spies into the land of Jericho. It was a critical time for the Israelites. After enduring so many hardships, they were due for some good things to happen. *"Then Joshua, son of Nun secretly sent two spies... 'Go, look over the land,' he said, 'especially Jericho'"* (Joshua 2:1).

It is an interesting point to fathom. God directed the spies to a land of unknowns, in particular, to a possible prostitute's home. Can you imagine what the spies were thinking? I believe when the Scripture says, *"So they went and entered the house of a prostitute named Rahab and stayed there"* (Joshua 2:1b) that the spies had heard about Rahab as they began their secret mission.

The gossip grapevine, even back then, would have been as it is today, fast and furious. I imagine the scoop in Jericho and its surrounding areas went something like this:

"Hey, did you hear about Rahab? She's not prostituting anymore. She's losing a lot of money. Some of the girls have quit too; not too sure why, but the men are fussing about it." I think the talk got back to the Israelites somehow.

Just a theory, but I think the spies knew the dangerous mission on which they were embarking. Could they really trust a prostitute with their lives? Nonetheless, God sent the two spies right up to Rahab's door.

It was a gutsy move she made. Her choice: She could have chose not to answer the door because of her shame due to all the men she had kept for more than 20 years. Or she could open the door and risk death. Despite Rahab's apparent misgivings of what lay ahead for her, she went ahead and opened the door.

Do you think anyone saw Rahab open her door to the two spies? Of course.

The king of Jericho was told, "Look! Some of the Israelites have come here tonight to spy out the land." So the king of Jericho sent this message to Rahab, "Bring out the men who came to you and entered your house, because they have come to spy out the whole land."
—Joshua 2:2–3

So much for an incognito mission. Notice what Rahab did. She lied straight through her teeth.

> *"Yes, the men came to me, but I did not know where they had come from. At dusk, when it was time to close the city gate, the men left. I don't know which way they went. Go after them quickly. You may catch up with them."*
> —Joshua 2:4–5

Now remember, this is coming from a prostitute who probably entertained a few of the king's men, not to mention perhaps the king himself. The king trusted Rahab's word because of her past. What? Yes, God used Rahab's shameful past to ultimately lead His children into the Promised Land. Think about it for a second. God took something that Satan delighted in, namely Rahab's occupation, and turned it into glory for His use!

Was it wrong of Rahab to lie? This is truly a complicated question. Shame could have kept Rahab from opening her door to the spies. Shame could have caused Rahab to turn the men over to the king, not to mention her fear. Why did Rahab do it? I believe she was just like us. She got sick of the shame, the hiding, and the secrecy.

Opening the door was a testimony of her invaluable newfound faith. Her door was literally a threshold of opportunity.

Have you ever been afraid of change?

I used to be afraid of change until I discovered that change exists for opportunities to present themselves each and every morning we get up out of bed.

Thus, this woman with the past longer than an arm is redeemed through that past.

How can—or has—God redeemed you through your past?

121

WEEK 5 • DAY 2
A THOUGHTFUL WOMAN

The men said to her, "This oath you made us swear will not be binding on us unless, when we enter the land, you have tied this scarlet cord in the window through which you let us down."
—Joshua 2:17–18

Let's look at Rahab's faith:

- First, her faith was embedded in courage. She opened the door when many of us would not have.
- Next, her faith was wise. She used her past to help God change the future for the Israelites.
- Then her faith was protective. She hid the spies in her home.
- There is one more detail that should not be overlooked. Rahab's faith was thoughtful.

Rahab's thoughtfulness meant she thought immediately to help spare her entire family from death. She expeditiously communicated to the spies what she wanted to happen after the spies went back to Joshua and later invaded Jericho. Faith is like that, you know. When the chips are down and the going gets tough, faith invests itself in those we love the most. Did not Jesus, as He was dying, think of His mother and ask John the disciple to care for her? Faith is courageous, wise, protective, and thoughtful. Shame forgets. Faith remembers.

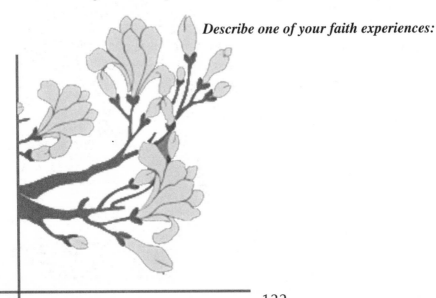

Describe one of your faith experiences:

It is important to note that God used Rahab just where she was. Literally and figuratively. She used her home, the home where the likelihood is that wedding vows were broken there, hearts crushed, and shame reigned in tis house. Rahab's house of shame became God's plane of glory, a literal haven for His kingdom and children.

Figuratively, God used Rahab where she was in her spiritual walk of faith. Had she been a believer long? No. Did she know the Four Spiritual Laws? No. Did she know the Sinner's Prayer? No. All Rahab knew was that she had to open the door that day. To get off that old wall just as Red got off that old dam.

Did you see the great detail of intimacy that God rendered for Rahab? Remember, Rahab has just asked the spies that her family be spared from death. See the heart of God at work here.

> *The men said to her, "This oath you made us swear will not be binding on us unless, when we enter the land, you have tied this scarlet cord in the window through which you let us down."*
> —Joshua 2:17–18

Can God use you right where you are?

There may be two reasons God specifically had the spies to demand a red cord in the window. First, God may have used the color of red blood to signify the Passover.

> *"On that same night I will pass through Egypt and strike down every firstborn— both men and animals—and I will bring judgment on all the gods of Egypt. I am the LORD. The blood will be a sign for you on the houses where you are; and when I see the blood, I will pass over you."*
> —Exodus 12:12–13a

Thus, the scarlet cord was verification and assurance for Rahab that she and her family would be spared from death.

The specific color was not an accident.

"For the life of a creature is in the blood, and I have given it to you to make atonement for yourselves on the altar; it is the blood that makes atonement for one's life."
—Leviticus 17:11

I believe God used this visual example for Rahab because she was struggling with fear and shame. Maybe like you and I, she did not feel worthy. Or perhaps she didn't feel totally forgiven. Since the life of a creature is in the blood, Rahab was forgiven due to the atonement of life represented in the blood.

Life comes after the blood. Just as God passed over the Israelites after they put the lamb's blood on their door, so too did God pass over Rahab's house after she let down the scarlet cord. *"And she tied the scarlet cord in the window"* (Joshua 2:21*b*). I believe God used this one last act of Rahab to signify to her that blood cleanses one's life. No longer was Rahab the prostitute, but instead she was the Jericho woman who helped the Israelites into the Promised Land and secured the lives of those in her household as well.

Secondly, God also used the scarlet cord to foreshadow the coming and purpose of Christ. Romans 5:9*a* says, *"We have now been justified by his blood."* Not only was Rahab justified by the blood, but she was *"redeemed by his blood"* (Ephesians 1:7*a*). Without this scarlet cord, Rahab would have been left to her self-doubt of shame. God, in His mercy and goodness, sent His most reassuring sign the color red, symbolizing the saving blood of sacrifice.

Describe how God has provided you with reassurance or write what reassurance you desire from Him:

The color red does not merely express justification found in blood, but also is depicted in the Bible as the color or representation of sin. *"Come now, let us reason together,"* says the Lord, *"Though your sins are like scarlet, they shall be as white as snow"* (Isaiah 1:18*a*). Isn't it stunning that God uses the color of red to turn Rahab from shame and sin to forgiveness and glory?

Did God really fathom Rahab's shame and need to overcome her past? I believe He did. After all, God Incarnate, Jesus Christ, was mocked by His persecutors. That is to say, they made fun of Jesus and His power to take away sin by *"stripping him and putting a scarlet robe on him"* (Matthew 27:28). By putting a scarlet robe on Christ—one that might be used to identify royalty—the Roman soldiers intended to shame Him. They mocked Him as though He could *not* take away sin, when in actuality He *could* and did. He who *"had no sin"* (2 Corinthians 5:21) endured the shame. What His enemies intended to mock Jesus actually symbolized His victory over shame and His true identity as King.

Rahab is counted in the genealogy of Christ; Ruth's mother-in-law and King David's ancestor. A prostitute who had once used her home to entertain men of all sorts won an eternal legacy in spite of her shame. Christ redeemed Rahab's house of shame to catapult her into a place of significance. Her story has been told from generation to generation as God Almighty turned her shame into His glory. Satan's doorway of sin became God's threshold of honor.

How might God use your shame to reveal His glory and how might He change—or has He already changed—your life to provide you with a position of worth in Him?

WEEK 5 • DAY 3
MARY'S BABY

"This is how the birth of Jesus Christ came about: His mother Mary was pledged to be married to Joseph, but before they came together, she was found to be with child through the Holy Spirit. Because Joseph her husband was a righteous man and did not want to expose her to public disgrace, he had in mind to divorce her quietly."
—Matthew 1:18–19

The fifth and final woman from the genealogy of Christ is Mary, mother of Jesus. Talk about a difficult assignment. Mary, a teenager (as was the marriage age back in that day) faced enormous shame while carrying the King of kings.

I'll go out on a limb here and venture a guess that the people back in Mary's time reacted the same way we would today—full of mockery, scorn, and disbelief.

You've got to be kidding. Sure. Yeah, right. Uh huh. Get out of here. Come on. Get real. You're full of it. That's right. Blame it on God Himself. Impregnated by God. Lock her up. Put on the straight jacket. Break open the medication. Can you imagine what the conversation would be and what would happen in today's world if a 15-year-old peasant girl or, in our case, a lower-income teen told authorities that the father of her baby was, well, you know, God? It would make front page headlines of course, but in a negative light.

What would your feelings have been if you had become pregnant and yet never had had sex?

What do you think Mary's family and friends thought of her at this point? What would you have done? How would you have treated Mary?

126

Some of us might argue that Mary felt no shame at all. After all, look at Mary's song of praise, or *Magnificat* in Luke 1, after the angel Gabriel told her that she would conceive God's Son by the Holy Spirit.

And Mary said, "My soul doth magnify the Lord,
And my spirit hath rejoiced in God my Saviour.
For he hath regarded the low estate of his handmaiden: for, behold, from hence-
forth all generations shall call me blessed.
For he that is mighty hath done to me great things; and holy is his name.
And his mercy is on them that fear him from generation to generation.
He hath shewed strength with his arm; he hath scattered the proud in the
imagination of their hearts.
He hath put down the mighty from their seats, and exalted them of low degree.
He hath filled the hungry with good things; and the rich he hath sent empty away.
He hath helped his servant Israel, in remembrance of his mercy;
As he spake to our fathers, to Abraham, and to his seed for ever."
—Luke 1:46–55 (KJV)

Clearly, Mary felt no shame at this point. But what about later? What about *after* the angel left? As tongues wagged fiercely in town, God merely watched and simply added Mary's name to the genealogy of Christ. Let's take a look at what happened after the angel left her.

Imagine being about 14 or 15 years old, engaged to be married, and having an angel appear and tell you that you will become pregnant by God (See Matthew 1:18). Imagine the words you would try to find in order to tell your parents you were carrying a child by God. "By the way, Mom and Dad, I haven't had sex yet, but I'm pregnant. No, really I am. It's never ever happened before, but I'm the one God has chosen to carry the Messiah, never to be done again."

As a parent, what would have been going through your mind?

127

I think it's awfully important that God told Mary's fiancé, Joseph, that Mary was pregnant as a virgin by the Holy Spirit in a dream (Matthew 1:23). When Joseph found out Mary was pregnant through the Holy Spirit, *"He decided he did not want to expose her to public disgrace, he had in mind to divorce her quietly"* (Matthew 1:19*b*). At first Joseph wanted out of the picture altogether. However, after the dream, Joseph decided to stay. God told Joseph that Mary's pregnancy was by the Holy Spirit so Mary wouldn't be alone, isolated, afraid, or ignorant about His redemptive plan.

It is interesting that Mary goes away to her cousin Elizabeth. Why on earth would Mary quickly run to Elizabeth?

God had told Mary about Elizabeth's miracle too. I think Mary quickly went to visit someone who was in a similar situation as her—her relative, Elizabeth, who carried Jesus's cousin, John the Baptist.

> *"At that time Mary got ready and hurried to a town in the hill country of Judea, where she entered Zechariah's home and greeted Elizabeth... Mary stayed with Elizabeth for about three months and then returned home."*
> —Luke 1:39–40; 56

Imagine what these two women did during the three months they were together. What might they have discussed, just as women discuss their lives today?

Since Elizabeth was carrying a godly child, filled with the Holy Spirit from conception (Luke 1:15*b*) she could empathize with Mary and the supernatural nature of their pregnancies.

The two women were close and obviously looked to each other for support. They both were facing similar circumstances. **However, why did Mary hurry there as the Scripture says?**

Might Mary also have wanted to escape the shame she felt in her hometown; the perceived shame of being pregnant out-of-wedlock?

What about the possible shame of rumors that she was crazy? The perceived shame of no one believing her except her fiancé and her relative, Elizabeth?

When have you felt shame over no one believing you about a situation?

How were you comforted?

Who comforted you?

WEEK 5 • DAY 4
A DAY OF STONING—ALMOST

And the angel said unto her, "Fear not, Mary: for thou hast found favour with God."
—Luke 1:30 (KJV)

Under Jewish law, the public could have judged and stoned Mary

If a man happens to meet in a town a virgin pledged to be married and he sleeps with her, you shall take both of them to the gate of that town and stone them to death—the girl because she was in a town and did not scream for help, and the man because he violated another man's wife. You must purge the evil from among you.
—Deuteronomy 22:23–24

Such was the fate of those women who went outside the bounds of their soon-to-be marriage and engaged in premarital sex. Ever wondered how such women who engaged in sex outside marriage found a more-than-willing crowd that wanted to do nothing more than to stone them? (See John 8:7.) Just think about it. Mary, virgin Mary, almost stoned to death. You may find it unfathomable, but in actuality she is in very good company, joining the Apostle Paul (2 Corinthians 11:25) and Stephen, the disciple (Acts 7:58a).

It should be noted here that Mary *"had found favor with God"* (Luke 1:30a NIV). Just why exactly did God choose Mary above all other women to carry His Son? First of all, I believe Mary was humble. How many of us would have wrongly thought we deserved to carry God Himself? But not Mary; she was a humble and sincere peasant teenager.

Secondly, Mary loved God and His commandments. If Mary were to support her husband, Joseph, in raising the Messiah, then God wanted to choose a mother who would have been devoted to the spiritual education of her children. Yes, Mary would have had to love God and His ways in order to support her husband as he taught the One who fulfilled the Scriptures. Talk about irony.

It would take a devoted mother and wife to reinforce the Scriptures with her children on a daily basis. Remember, by age 12, Jesus was in the temple amazing t h e scholars (Luke 2:49). God had to have looked down and smiled. After all, it was in His divine plan to have an out-of-wedlock pregnant teenager rearing His Son, King of kings and Lord of lords, who confounded the teachers of the Law in the temple. Who do you think helped to prepared Him for such a task? Yes, a humble, devoted, and Scripture-obeying young person.

Think about it. A girl, of today's standard, in about the ninth grade. Ponytail. Braces. Getting ready to take her driver's test. A giggly teenager. That's today's picture. God chose Mary, who would be considered a mere babe in today's world, to minister to God be Son Himself, a virtual newborn. Should this not be enough to stop the critics who look down on young mothers? No, we're not promoting teen pregnancy or out-of-wedlock pregnancy. Rather, the Word challenges us to build up today's mothers as well as youth and to invite them into the spiritual heritage they deserve.

Do you look down on younger women?

What do the youth of today offer to the world?

For example, Paul admonished Timothy to *"not let anyone look down on you because you are young, but set an example for the believers in speech, in life, in love, in faith, and in purity"* (1 Timothy 5:11*b*–12). I think today in the church many times we ignore the young people based solely on their age—never mind their gifts of singing, evangelism, service, and so on.

If you are a young woman, does this encourage you? How?

If you are an older woman, how does this encourage you?

What woman or women can you share this encouragement with to build them up in love?

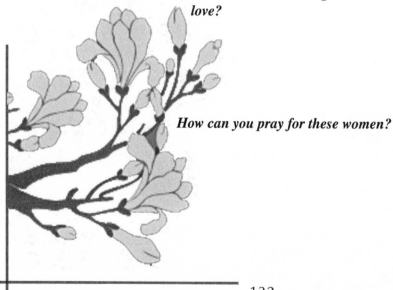

How can you pray for these women?

WEEK 5 • DAY 5
GOD'S MESSENGERS

"Elijah was a man just like us."
—James 5:17*a*

I recently sat down on a Friday night and watched an intriguing show centered around a high school student named Joan. In the show, God chose to appear to her at any given moment in the bodily form of any given person. He talked to her as another student, a trash man, a salesperson, and so on. But the mere fact that the show highlights the theme that God chooses to use His methods through a teen is exciting. The show mirrors the fact that God uses young people, such as Mary, the mother of Christ, to literally deliver His divine message. He can use anyone.

Tamar, Rahab, Ruth, Bathsheba, and Mary. Three sexually impure women. One codependent widow. One teenybopper. Make no mistakes about it. God handpicked these people out of all the other more socially accepted women He could have chosen. Did they have their lives all together? No. Were they religiously correct in all their theology? Probably not. Surely God could have done it all more properly. True.

Why did God use the people He used?

Why can God use you?

How has God worked through you?

How might God work through you?

God has used these women in Jesus's genealogy to give us, His imperfect people, a hope. For us to take to heart that *"Elijah was a man just like us"* (James 5:17a). To tell us that if He can use them, in their humanness, then surely He can use us for His divine purpose and plan.

Want more proof that God uses the shamed? Starting next week, we will study several other biblical examples of how God uses people, women in these instances, to turn their shame for His glory. We've seen the genealogy, now let's dig deeper.

My Prayer

Dear Lord, we have seen the five women in the genealogy of Christ, such imperfect women, who You used to carry out Your divine message. They were not perfect. They didn't have it all together. Ultimately, they had one thing in common. Honesty. I believe they were honest with You. The only prerequisite You give.

Help us to be totally honest. The good, the bad, and yes, the ugly. The addictions, the desperation, the failures. I abandon myself to You, for You alone are the Giver and Perfecter of Life. You alone are in charge of changing me.

Help me to get out of the way so You can do what You have always done; change my life. In Jesus's name, Amen.

Your Prayer

PART 3

Shameless

Scorning the Shame Forever

The Samaritan Woman
and A Sinful Woman

When a Samaritan woman came to draw water, Jesus said to her, "Will you give me a drink?"
—John 4:7*b*

"Your sins are forgiven."
—Luke 7:50*b*

Darkness veiled the never-ending shame engulfed deep within these women's minds, souls, and bodies. Always lurking around the corner, shame seldom ventured far from its home in their hearts. Shame vacillated on their tightrope of self-hatred and anger. As if on cue, shame presented itself at the most inopportune times—leaving these women to grapple with its flashes of brilliant deceit, battling them. Only through Christ's redemption would these women gain the nerve to defeat shame's ploys against them.

WEEK 6 • DAY 1
A DAY OF DARKNESS

It was about the sixth hour...a Samaritan woman came to draw water.
—John 4:6*b*

Defeated. She had been there. Lived there. She had a past; everyone does.

What comes to mind when you think of your past?

I have a theory. It's not a complex theory, mind you, just a guess that I have. I believe that when we are thirsty, we are at our humblest in terms of need. Have you ever seen a person, thirsty for anything, offered a drink, and watched them gulp the liquid down? It is a humbling sight to behold. We all need water. Our bodies crave it. It's good for us. And yet, some of us deny the very thing that facilitates our good health.

We hate what we were made for. It is as though we cannot stand to be needy in search of what God created us to desire. Living water. Perhaps the woman at the well yearned for this. Her parched tongue agonized for a single drop of compassion. Tenderness. Respect. Is it any wonder that Christ Himself offered not only this woman at the well living water (John 4:10) but to others as well (John 7:38).

The Samaritan woman at the well battled shame on a daily basis. How do I know this? That's easy. She went everyday at noon to draw water from the well. *"It was about the sixth hour…a Samaritan woman came to draw water"* (John 4:6b). She needed water everyday. It was *life-giving* to her, but her life itself seemed *lifeless*.

Her shame prohibited her from getting water when all the other women do. It was customary that women went to Jacob's well in the evening, when it was cooler. Not so for the Samaritan woman. Have you ever been so ashamed that you avoided people altogether? I have. I let my shame reign supreme and would go to the grocery store at the oddest hours—hours when no one would see me. What was I so ashamed of? Simply put, I was ashamed of being me. Can you relate?

What have you been so ashamed of that you might avoid others at all cost?

Now he had to go through Samaria. So he came to a town in Samaria called Sychar, near the plot of ground Jacob had given to his son Joseph. Jacob's well was there, and Jesus, tired as he was from the journey, sat down by the well. It was about the sixth hour.

When a Samaritan woman came to draw water, Jesus said to her, "Will you give me a drink?" (His disciples had gone into the town to buy food.)

The Samaritan woman said to him, "You are a Jew and I am a Samaritan woman. How can you ask me for a drink?" (For Jews do not associate with Samaritans.)

Jesus answered her, "If you knew the gift of God and who it is that asks you for a drink, you would have asked him and he would have given you living water."

"Sir," the woman said, "you have nothing to draw with and the well is deep. Where can you get this living water? Are you greater than our father Jacob, who gave us the well and drank from it himself, as did also his sons and his flocks and herds?"

Jesus answered, "Everyone who drinks this water will be thirsty again, but whoever drinks the water I give him will never thirst. Indeed, the water I give him will become in him a spring of water welling up to eternal life."

The woman said to him, "Sir, give me this water so that I won't get thirsty and have to keep coming here to draw water."
—John 4:4–15

You see, the woman at the well had needs. Deep needs that had been left unfulfilled. She had been married and divorced several times and the man she was currently living with when she met Jesus for the first time was not actually her *husband* (John 4:17). Thus, she looked to relationships to fill the void or emptiness in her life, but it was to no avail. Perhaps Jesus comes to her at a pivotal time in her life. She feels defeated. Alone. Afraid. Lost. Just for a Jewish man to interact with a Samaritan woman publicly was unfathomable during that biblical time period. However, Jesus always goes where the hurting are found. He travels down into the trenches. Into the bleakness. Into the dark hearts—then and now. Watch carefully as the Master works. It is a sight to behold.

We know the Samaritan woman felt enormous shame because she went to the well at the hottest time of the day when no other women were around. Watch the irony here as the King prepared this broken woman's heart to receive His compassion. Christ asks the Samaritan woman for a drink. *"Jesus said to her, 'Will you give me a drink?'"* (John 4:7b). Imagine that the Living Water Himself, Jesus, asked this poor, shamed, outcast for a drop of replenishment. We could debate with scholars over why Jesus did this. I think the answer is a simple one. He was thirsty. Would she ignore the religious customs of the day and interact with Him? *"You are a Jew and I am a Samaritan woman. How can you ask me for a drink?" (For Jews did not associate with Samaritans)* (John 4:9).

Perhaps Jesus wanted to drive home the point that He was asking her for a drink when in actuality she was dying of spiritual and emotional thirst. *"Jesus answered her, "If you knew the gift of God and who it is that asks you for a drink, you would have asked him and he would have given you living water"* (John 4:10).

The Samaritan woman answers Christ with a candid reply. *"Sir, you have nothing to draw with and the well is too deep. Where can you get this living water?"* (John 4:11,) It is as though she was telling Jesus that He did not possess the tools in which to help her fulfill and meet her deepest longings. However, notice after she told Jesus that He did not have anything to draw with and that in essence her "well," or life were too deep, or too tattered, that she said, *"Where can you get this living water?"* (v. 11b) Thus, she still held out some sense of hope.

Don't we, as children of God, hold onto the fantasy that one day, indeed, our Prince will come to get us, redeem us, and rid us of all our shame. One day the revolving door of shame will cease to turn and our Hope, Jesus, will replace that cyclical shame with a doorway of opportunity. Yes, the woman at the well held out hope in the midst of defeat.

Do you wonder whether God "has the tools"—whether He is able to quench your thirst; emotional, physical, spiritual?

Week 6 • Day 2
The Day of Past

"Everyone who drinks this water will be thirsty again, but whoever drinks this water I give him will never thirst. Indeed, the water I give him will become in him a spring of water welling up to eternal life."
—John 4:13–14

Then Jesus told her, no holding back, what He had to offer—not what the world of shame offers its victims. Jesus said, *"Indeed, the water I give him will become in him a spring of water welling up to eternal life."*

The Samaritan woman grabbed onto this offer with all she had. *"Sir, give me this water so that I won't get thirsty and have to keep coming here to draw water"* (John 4:15) In effect, she was pleading with everything she has to be rid of her shame. Her past. Her sins. She despised coming each day to the well, only to be reminded of her overwhelming shame. Each day she came, she was reminded of the separation between her and the other women. She was an orphan of sorts. No family to cling to hold. No friends to clasp onto for fellowship. Just an old heavy millstone tied around her neck that drowned her every fiber in a sea of regrettable shame.

Notice carefully what Jesus did next. He tests her honesty. *"Go, call your husband and come back"* (John 4:16). The Samaritan woman answered, *"I have no husband"* (John 4:17) Jesus went on to tell her that she was right and that she had had several husbands, five to be exact, and that the current man she was living with was not even her legal husband (John 4:18). Thus, the past was out in the open. No more dark corners for her shame to crawl or creep into.

Isn't that what God desires in us, truth in the inmost places of our hearts? To finally come face to face with our own humanness and frailty?

What is the inmost truth about your situation that you want to share with Jesus?

Christ goes on to tell this woman eventually that He is the Messiah (John 4:26). This is the only place where Jesus directly admitted to being the Messiah except at His trial (Mark 9:41). Isn't it stunning that Jesus hand-picked this woman, a woman whom society might deem a whore, to reveal His identity to? Surely there were more deserving women out there.

Out of all the people He could have chosen, why do you think Jesus chose the Samaritan woman to know His identity?

Notice what the Samaritan woman did. She left *"her water jar and went back to the town and said to the people, 'Come, see a man who told me everything I ever did'"* (John 4:28). Overjoyed at the prospect of having encountered the long-awaited Messiah, this despised, divorced, and sexually impure woman went all over the town that once shunned her to tell them the good news of Christ. What changed this woman? Rather, it was *who* changed this woman at the well?

Is your "well" too deep, as the woman at the well told Christ hers was? How so?

Think your past nullifies you from becoming worthy in God's eyes? Why?

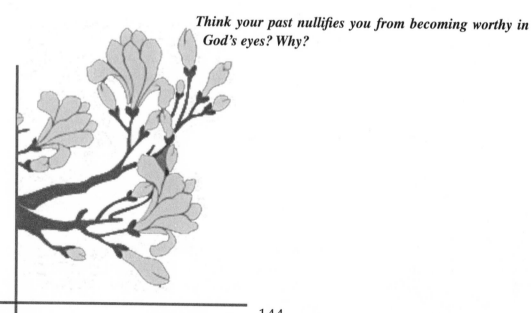

WEEK 6 • DAY 3
A DAY OF DISCOVERY

One of the Pharisees asked Jesus to have dinner with him, so Jesus went to his home and sat down to eat. When a certain immoral woman from that city heard he was eating there, she brought a beautiful alabaster jar filled with expensive perfume. Then she knelt behind him at his feet, weeping. Her tears fell on his feet, and she wiped them off with her hair. Then she kept kissing his feet and putting perfume on them.

When the Pharisee who had invited him saw this, he said to himself, "If this man were a prophet, he would know what kind of woman is touching him. She's a sinner!"

Then Jesus answered his thoughts. "Simon," he said to the Pharisee, "I have something to say to you."

"Go ahead, Teacher," Simon replied.

Then Jesus told him this story: "A man loaned money to two people—500 pieces of silver to one and 50 pieces to the other. But neither of them could repay him, so he kindly forgave them both, canceling their debts. Who do you suppose loved him more after that?"

Simon answered, "I suppose the one for whom he canceled the larger debt."

"That's right," Jesus said. Then he turned to the woman and said to Simon, "Look at this woman kneeling here. When I entered your home, you didn't offer me water to wash the dust from my feet, but she has washed them with her tears and wiped them with her hair. You didn't greet me with a kiss, but from the time I first came in, she has not stopped kissing my feet. You neglected the courtesy of olive oil to anoint my head, but she has anointed my feet with rare perfume.

"I tell you, her sins—and they are many—have been forgiven, so she has shown me much love. But a person who is forgiven little shows only little love." Then Jesus said to the woman, "Your faith has saved you; go in peace."
—Luke 7:36–50 (NLT)

This scene took place at a dinner party at the home of a Pharisee. While dining with the religious elite, a sinful woman, or prostitute, approached Jesus with an alabaster jar of perfume. Notice here Jesus's response to this sinful woman. Christ does not stop her and say, "You are too sinful to come to me; wait a while and I might not be as angry then." No, the God of all comfort graciously lets sin approach Him. Nothing is too unclean for Him.

The woman found out Jesus would be in town and she went to him. Was she scared to death? Of course. Was she forbidden from entering the Pharisee's house according to Jewish custom? Yes.

What was it that drove this woman to take her valuable perfume, only later to break it and pour it on Jesus's feet?

What was the Pharisee's reaction?

What was Jesus's reaction?

How can you relate your answers to your own situation?

I have often wondered why the woman dried Jesus's feet with her hair. Surely she could have brought a cloth along with her. But you see, that is not what true love does. Anointing Jesus was a desperate act of love. On impulse, she took the expensive perfume and literally ran to the Pharisee's home. There, she interrupted the flow of events and tries to communicate her heartfelt cry for help to Him. Is He the Son of God? Can He heal her and her past? It is as though she risked everything on the One who could set her free from her shame.

What kind of shame did she bring to the table? Well, being a woman of the veil, or prostitute, she engaged in premarital sex as well as adultery. Did you see Jesus's response to her shame? He forgave her.

While others around us may judge us and condemn us for the many past sins in our lives, Christ understands the desperation we feel to rid ourselves of shame.

It wasn't the religious leaders who forgave this woman, but rather Christ alone. Did God silence her after she came to Him? No, He did just the opposite. He told her to go in peace. Christ empathized with her. He Himself would later bear the shame of the Cross.

Like this woman, many of us have choices. After Christ told her that her sins were forgiven, that her faith had healed her, and to go in peace (Luke 7:48, 50), she had two options. One, she could take her newfound conversion and have been enslaved to the shame of her past life. The other alternative was to abandon herself totally to Christ and hold onto Him for her worth.

Which option would you choose or have you chosen?

WEEK 6 • DAY 4
A REALITY OF HEAVEN

"Go in peace."
—Luke 7:50

Imagine with me, if you will, two conversations. One is in the Pharisee's house while the other is in the throne room of heaven.

"Why, did you see that whore barging in here and interrupting our meal? She touched Jesus and didn't even bother to change her prostitute clothes. She was not presentable in our presence. Nothing but a slut."

Now listen to God: "Yes, come as you are, for I see what you really are, My child. Your shame is now my glory."

So many of us let our past interfere with our present and, therefore, our future in Christ.

Do the past sins of yesteryear cause unspeakable shame that excludes you from being all God has called you to be?

Many of us know our sins are forgiven, but do we *"go in peace"* as God commanded this unnamed woman? The choices we make today, this instant, determine how we see Christ. Is He truly our Deliverer, or do we fall victim to the spell of disbelief?

For many years, I knew intellectually that God had forgiven me. However, in my heart of hearts, I didn't feel forgiven—due to the *shame*. A friend once explained how to overcome this. Say you wake up one morning and just don't feel like a woman. Then you go into the bathroom, shower, and get ready for the day. Sure enough, even though you don't *feel* like a woman, the truth is that you *are*. Feelings are perhaps the toughest part of shame altogether. Many times they are the last component to fall into line with God's truth.

We live in a society that says you must dress up salvation. That is, we want to clean it up, so to speak. We play by the rules that say, "You can't wear that and walk down the aisle to be saved." Why not? Didn't God handpick certain people to go and tell the others He was alive? What if they had decided to clean themselves up before approaching Christ? Perhaps the sense of urgency to cling to Him would have been overshadowed by their shame.

If we truly believe anyone can be saved from their sins through Christ, then we should be appalled, flabbergasted, shocked...and hopeful. To say that no one is so far removed from the grace of God is a scary thought. This inherently creates an ideology with which many Christians are uncomfortable. I call it equality at the Cross.

For thousands of years, there has been a not so subtle division of the classes. Call it what you may, but the fact remains that there is an all-too-obvious class distinction in virtually all corners of the world.

What would you, as a Christian, think of a prostitute coming down your church aisle in her miniskirt, spiked heels, and fishnet stockings, not to mention her low-cut blouse?

Needless to say, it would be uncomfortable for many onlookers. But you see, the Cross *is* an uncomfortable place. It it the place where everyone is equal in God's eyes. *Everyone has worth. Everyone can come to Christ as they are.* What better example to see this demonstrated than in this unnamed prostitute?

What about the our equality at the Cross comforts you?

What about it makes you uncomfortable?

Week 6 • Day 5
Being Who God Created Us to Be

"Come unto me."

What is it that we, as women, have learned from the women we have studied? First, we can come to Christ as we are. There is no need to clean up our sins before we come. He is not a dictator in the sky who becomes more loving with time. No, no matter when we come to Him, He is ready to comfort us.

What other lessons do you see?

Are you trying to "fix" yourself before you come to Jesus Christ with your issues?

We must believe, as these women did, that Christ alone is the answer. We put our faith not only in churches, pastors, or religious leaders, but rather first and foremost in Jesus. God can truly transform a life of shame into His glory.

Next, we can give Him *what* we can *when* we can. Notice that one woman bought an alabaster jar of perfume for Christ. Sure, she could have saved up and bought something prettier or more expensive, but she did what she could then, not later. God desires we come now to Him, regardless of how we look or what we have to bring or don't bring to Him. The woman in Luke 7 gave her gift as a desperate act of love that came from her heart. And isn't the heart what God is interested in the most?

One look. That is all it took. No lectures. No sermons. No name-calling. She only brought her most honest feelings and emotions. And with one look she went from a woman of shame into a woman of glory. She simply took God at His Word. We would be wise to follow her example. All it takes is one look from the Master.

Join the Bible women today and get rid of the shame. Replace bad shame with the truth that we are accepted and that we are winners and children of the King of kings!

Are you ready to experience the redemption of Jesus Christ and the freedom He has for you daily?

So far, all the biblical women we've studied have had major issues. Major pasts. Major sins. Major doubts. Major shame and need for redemption. However, there is one common thread in their tapestry of life: honesty. They are honest beyond measure. Instead of stuffing their feelings, they freely flung their truth to the wind. And God, the Windmaster, carried their truth on the soaring wings of His dawn.

Together, coupled with their pain and shame, they were molded in His image. Yes, these women of the Bible have looked and lived shame as you and I have. They knew the pain we experience—of going to the grocery store at 5 A.M. They knew the shame of being afraid of unmentionable memories. Can you relate? Hang in there. Help is on the way. Thirsty for healing? Then read on. God truly desires to release the floodgates of the living waters. God's deepest longing? To meet us where we are, like He did for the woman at the well, the women in the Pharisee's house, and to satisfy us.

My Prayer

Dear Lord, my well is deep and my tongue is parched for water, Your water. Give me what I need, life sustaining water so I can tell others about You. There is no one too sinful, too deep, to drink from You. Make me thirsty for You, for You are that water. Help me to seek You out instead of something else to fill me—drugs, alcohol, sex, codependency, eating disorders, or anything else. Open Your floodgates of heaven and pour out Your healing touch today, whether that is a friend, your Word, a psychiatrist, a therapist, a card of encouragement, or a simple prayer. I will try my best to be water to others, but first I need You to be water to me. In Jesus's name, Amen.

Your Prayer

On the Fringe of Wholeness

Mary Magdalene and the Woman Who Bled

"If... I will be healed."
—Mark 5:28*b*

WEEK 7 • DAY 1
A FLOOD OF EMOTIONS

Throughout the gospels, Mary Magdalene's intimate spiritual relationship with the Savior Jesus Christ is evident.

> *Near the cross of Jesus stood his mother, his mother's sister, Mary the wife of Clopas, and Mary Magdalene.*
> *—John 19:25*

It is worth emphasizing that Mary Magdalene was not a prostitute—though Jesus could have healed her from this abuse and injustice if she were—but for centuries has born this moniker due to wrong interpretation of her role in biblical history; she has been associated with the woman in Luke 7:36–50. Mary Magdalene's significance to Jesus's ministry was for other reasons. She was, in fact, another one of Jesus's walking miracles.

"She appears before us for the first time in Luke 8:2 among the women who 'ministered unto him of their substance.' All appear to have occupied a position of comparative

wealth. With all the chief motive was that of gratitude for their deliverance from 'evil spirits and infirmities.' Of Mary it is said specially that 'seven devils went out of her,' and the number indicates a possession of more than ordinary malignity. She was present during the closing hours of the agony on the cross. (John 19:25) She remained by the cross till all was over, and waited till the body was taken down and placed in the garden sepulchre of Joseph of Arimathaea, (Matthew 27:61; Mark 15:47; Luke 23:55) when she, with Salome and Mary the mother of James, 'bought sweet spices that they might come and anoint' the body. (Mark 16:1) The next morning accordingly, in the earliest dawn, (Matthew 28:1; Mark 16:2) they came with Mary the mother of James to the sepulchre. Mary Magdalene had been to the tomb and had found it empty, and had seen the 'vision of angels.' (Matthew 28:5; Mark 16:6) To her first of all Jesus appeared after his resurrection. (John 20:14,15) Mary Magdalene has become the type of a class of repentant sinners; but there is no authority for identifying her with the 'sinner' who anointed the feet of Jesus in (Luke 7:36–50) neither is there any authority for the supposition that Mary Magdalene is the same as the sister of Lazarus."
—www.bible.org

Though Mary was not a prostitute, she had her own set of issues—we know not what type—before coming into relationship with Christ.

What issues continue to plague you? Are these issues too hard for God to address?

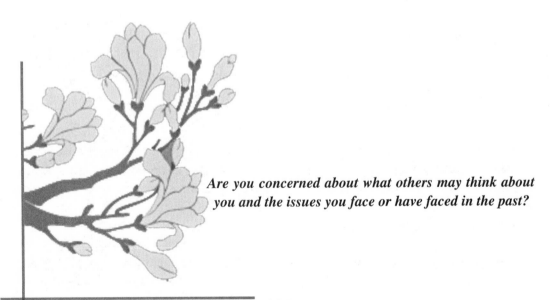

Are you concerned about what others may think about you and the issues you face or have faced in the past?

How do you believe God wants to help you to deal with these issues?

Do you need to seek others' support in the process? Who might you contact, in order to gain the godly support you need?

Mary must have been afraid; she had been possessed by *seven* demons. She probably had heard voices and had seen frightening images. She had been an outcast, surely marginalized by her condition. Everyone had told her she had demons. She had been drowning in shame—until Jesus came.

I imagine that some of her friends tried to help Mary. One of them may even have told her about a man travelling in the region of her village, Magdala, in Galilee, who was becoming increasingly popular in that He could heal people who had any kind of disease—including demoniacs. His name was Jesus.

Mary decided to go to Galilee. What could it hurt? She stood in the crowd, possibly convulsing. Maybe everyone stepped away from her. Everyone, that is, except Jesus.

Jesus stooped, eye-to-eye with this woman. He touched what no one else had touched her spirit. He cast out all the demons from Mary. She was healed. And Jesus told her she was healed her and forgiven of her sins.

What did Mary choose to do in order to be healed?

How does this apply to us today?

Soon afterward Jesus began a tour of the nearby towns and villages, preaching and announcing the Good News about the Kingdom of God. He took his twelve disciples with him, along with some women who had been cured of evil spirits and diseases. Among them were Mary Magdalene, from whom he had cast out seven demons; Joanna, the wife of Chuza, Herod's business manager; Susanna; and many others who were contributing their own resources to support Jesus and his disciples.
—Luke 8:1–3

We now see Mary identified as one of the women who traveled with Jesus's disciples. Mary Magdalene could not have forgotten the compassion Jesus had shown her when He told her she was forgiven. He had looked at her as no other human had looked at her—with a heart full of love. Mary had to follow this Man. Jesus had touched her soul, and she had come alive. She had a reason to live!

Mary's life makes it clear that Jesus can heal us completely and that He is not at all concerned about our past, except that our past *equips* us to be useful in ministering to others. It is worth repeating; our experiences and His healing give us power to help others overcome their shame for God's glory! Mary Magdalene, who had had seven demons cast out of her, went into ministry with Jesus, the Son of God, and His disciples—along with other women. All of these women had issues of some sort as did each of the men who followed Jesus.

Did Jesus say to Mary, or any of the other men or women who followed Him, as we see in Luke 8:1–3, "You need to grow and mature in your walk with me before I can really use you in my ministry"? No. Does Scripture record that Jesus told Mary Magdalene, "Go back to your home in Magdala and come see Me when you are ready"? No. Did Jesus make Mary jump through hoops in order to deem her worthy or did He ask a group of others to vouch for Mary Magdalene? No.

I sometimes think that the church looks down on new believers because they are not seasoned Christians. Many churches unfortunately will not let new believers participate fully until they have learned all the ins-and-outs of the faith. But look at the heart of God. Jesus allowed this Mary Magdalene to not only anoint Him, but also to travel with Him.

Mary was there when Jesus pursued His ministry. Mary was there when He rode a little donkey into Jerusalem. And

Mary was there when they nailed Him to the Cross.

Out of the millions of people Jesus could have appeared to after His resurrection, He chose to appear to an ex-demoniac. All it took was one look from Jesus. All it took was experiencing His healing presence.

Early on the first day of the week, while it was still dark, Mary Magdalene went to the tomb and saw that the stone had been removed from the entrance. So she came running to Simon Peter and the other disciple, the one Jesus loved, and said, "They have taken the Lord out of the tomb, and we don't know where they have put him!"

Then the disciples went back to their homes, but Mary stood outside the tomb crying. As she wept, she bent over to look into the tomb and saw two angels in white, seated where Jesus' body had been, one at the head and the other at the foot.

They asked her, "Woman, why are you crying?"

"They have taken my Lord away," she said, "and I don't know where they have put him." At this, she turned around and saw Jesus standing there, but she did not realize that it was Jesus.

"Woman," he said, "why are you crying? Who is it you are looking for?"

Thinking he was the gardener, she said, "Sir, if you have carried him away, tell me where you have put him, and I will get him."

Jesus said to her, "Mary."

She turned toward him and cried out in Aramaic, "Rabboni!" (which means Teacher).

Jesus said, "Do not hold on to me, for I have not yet returned to the Father. Go instead to my brothers and tell them, 'I am returning to my Father and your Father, to my God and your God.' "

Mary Magdalene went to the disciples with the news: "I have seen the Lord!" And she told them that he had said these things to her.
—John 20:1–2, 10–18

Could one look from Jesus really transform a life? It did Mary Magdalene's. Mary does not appear in Jesus's genealogy, but she forever changed when a carpenter from Nazareth showed up. She became as significant as any other follower of Jesus and His ministry.

Who did Christ appear to first after the Resurrection? A disciple? A religious leader? A family member?

God resoundingly chose a healed woman to see Himself first after He rose from the dead. Why on earth would God do this?

Have you discovered your purpose in life?

Christ's actions give us hope. God's Word lets us know that no one's shame is too great for the King of kings and Lord of lords. Mary's life makes it obvious that Jesus can heal us completely and that He is not concerned at all about our past, except where our past can equip us to be useful in ministering to others.

God is not concerned about our inadequacies. He has provided the cleansing blood of Jesus Christ to wash away our sins, to heal our hearts, minds, souls, and to give us His strength. It is worth repeating that our experiences and His healing give us power to help others overcome their shame—and we, therefore, do not get the glory. It is all to God's glory.

Remember, Mary Magdalene had seven demons cast out of her, and then went into ministry with Jesus and His disciples, along with other select women.

Among them were Mary Magdalene, from whom he had cast out seven demons; Joanna, the wife of Chuza, Herod's business manager; Susanna; and many others who were contributing their own resources to support Jesus and his disciples.
—Luke 8:1–3

158

WEEK 7 • DAY 2
THE REALITY OF SUFFERING

"Is any suffering like my suffering."
—Lamentations 1:12*b*

She had grown weary of the same condition day after day. Month after month. Year after year. She had endured the same disease for 12 long years. She had been bleeding for that many years. She was an outcast not only from society as a whole, but also on the level of family and friends. Simply put, she was ceremonially unclean from everything.

What does Leviticus 15:25–27 say?

Even if this woman was cured, what does Leviticus 15:28–30 say she had to do?

Read and record your impressions of Leviticus 15:31:

We know the woman who bled for 12 years suffered because Scripture tells us she did. In your own words, record what Mark 5:25–26 says.

What kind of emotional state would you be in if you spent all your money on doctors and yet you only got worse each year? Have you or someone you know faced this?

How would you feel if you had been shunned by everyone for more than a decade? It was customary for any woman who bled to be ceremonially unclean. The woman who bled for 12 years was an outcast; shamed because of her bleeding condition. There was practically no hope or help for her. She suffered a shaming disease and she suffered alone.

Do you think the future looked bright for this woman? Why or why not?

What would you have done if you had been her?

In your own words define the word outcast*:*

According to *The American Heritage Dictionary, outcast* is defined as "one who has been excluded from a society or system."

The woman who bled for 12 years was excluded from society. According to Leviticus 15:30, even if her bleeding stopped, she would then have to offer a sin offering to and through the priest. Sin offerings, according to Scripture had to take place outside the camp.

Record what Leviticus 4:12 and Leviticus 16:27 required:

Now record what Hebrews 13:11–13 says:

It is ironic that Christ, whose blood was shed, suffered outside the city as our sin offering. The woman who bled for 12 years suffered outside society and was not deemed worthy to be included in society. Jesus knew all about suffering outside the bounds of society.

What did this woman and Christ have in common?

What do you have in common with Christ?

It should be noted that although the woman who bled for 12 years suffered outside of society, she went into the city where Jesus was at the time to follow the crowd that had gathered around Jesus (Mark 5:24*b*). Both Jesus and this woman knew the importance of blood, and both also knew the shame of being deemed unworthy to be accepted in society.

Isn't it unfathomable that God Himself takes a shamed woman, the woman who bled for 12 years, and chooses her and her condition (bleeding) and accepts her when no one else would? Was Christ familiar with suffering? Oh yes, it was a reality He knew all too well. Sometimes it is just comforting knowing God knows exactly how we feel. Take heart friend; Christ knows our shame and all the other feelings of suffering we have experienced. He experienced being an outcast just as the woman who bled for 12 years did.

> *"He was despised and rejected by men, a man of sorrows, and familiar with suffering"*
> —Isaiah 53:3*a*

Week 7 • Day 3
The Edge of His Cloak

"She said to herself, If I only touch his cloak, I will be healed."
—Matthew 9:21

A thread. A fringe. A hair. She was at the point of desperation. She had heard about Jesus healing all sorts of diseases and interacting with those society shunned (Mark 5:27a). She had tried everything. Tried all the doctors. Now, after 12 long years, she was getting worse. She had made up her mind. Jesus was in the region of Decapolis, near Capernaum, when she saw the crowd. She decided to go for it; never mind the looks of disgust as her clothes were stained with blood. People were crowding the One called Jesus. She believed in her heart that this miracle worker could heal her. It couldn't hurt to touch the edge of His cloak, could it?

Record your impressions of what Mark 5:27–28 says:

Did this woman have faith? Why or why not?

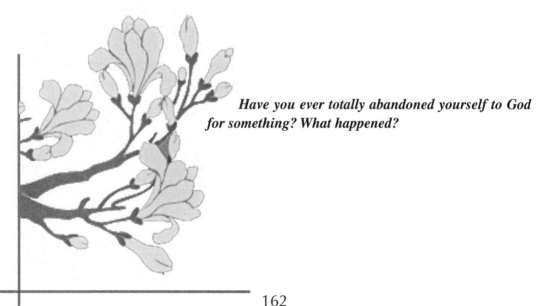

Have you ever totally abandoned yourself to God for something? What happened?

It was no small matter to push her way through the crowd and to come up behind Jesus. Yes, she was afraid. Yes, the crowd probably looked down on her because of all the blood on her clothes. Yes, everyone knew she was ceremonially unclean. More than anything she wanted to be rid of all the shame.

Record your thoughts about what Mark 5:29 says:

How quickly was she healed?

Has your faith ever been rewarded immediately? What was the result?

Notice that the phrase *"freed from her suffering"* is used (Mark 5:29b). God wants us to know that shame can imprison us with chains and bind us to a life of suffering, such as was the case of the woman who bled for 12 years. So, when God healed this woman, she was set free from her life of suffering. No longer was this woman an outcast. Free to be a part of a society, a community, a family, and friendships. This is what Christ can do for all of us who have faith in Him…if we just will touch the edge of His cloak, so to speak.

"Then you will know the truth, and the truth will set you free" (John 8:32). The Bible says that *"Immediately her bleeding stopped and she felt in her body that she was freed from her suffering"* (Mark 5:29).

Sometimes we want to be certain if something has taken place. Jesus knew this predicament. Was the woman who bled for 12 years healed? She felt she was. Yet Jesus confirmed this fact in a very unusual way.

Record what Jesus does in Mark 5:30:

How do His disciples respond to this in Mark 5:31?

Why do Jesus's remarks seem so outlandish?

Does Jesus give up or keep on insisting on knowing who touched Him?

Why do you think He does this in Mark 5:32?

Jesus could very easily have ignored the power that had gone out of Him, but He didn't. I believe He did this for two reasons. First of all, He wanted the woman who had bled to know beyond a shadow of a doubt that she had been healed. Scripture says she felt she was healed. Next, He wanted to validate the truth publicly.

What does Mark 5:33 say?

Was she scared to go forth?

What physical position did she take?

Why didn't this woman just ignore Jesus?

Scripture says she told Him *the whole truth*. She could have told Jesus it was her and then left. But she didn't.

What do you think she told Him?

I believe the woman who bled for 12 years confessed to
Jesus that she had bled for more than a decade and been deemed
ceremonially unclean. I also think she told Him how she had spent all her
money on doctors and instead of getting better, she had gotten worse. And one more thing:
I think she told Christ about the shame. She told Him everything that related to her disease
or sickness. She told him the whole truth.

It is interesting that Jesus, being God, knew this woman had been healed, and yet
He was adamant about wanting to know who had touched Him. Not only did Jesus desire
that the woman know she had been healed, but He wanted others to know as well. It was as
much a testament to others who He had healed as it was to this woman.

WEEK 7 • DAY 5
HEALING THAT SAVES

> *"It is Jesus's name and the faith that comes through him that has given this complete healing."*
> —Acts 3:16*b*

There are significant healings and then there are extraordinary healings. Make no bones
about it. This healing was extraordinary. If you had bled every day for 12 years, you would
consider the stopping of it a huge deal. Jesus's words to this woman were equally as important as the healing. Look at what He said; "Daughter, your faith has healed you. Go in peace
and be freed from your suffering" (Mark 5:34).

First of all, He called her an endearing term (daughter.) Why did Jesus do this?

Jesus very easily could have just called her "woman." But He did not. I believe He called
her "daughter" to let her know she was special to Him; to calm her fear after she fearfully
told Him the whole truth.

Has anyone ever called you a special name that meant a lot to you? Please explain:

Next, Jesus commended this woman's faith. Define faith *in your own words:*

Faith, in this example, can be defined as belief or trust. Jesus commended this woman for her trust in Him or belief in Him. It is interesting to note that the Greek word used for "healed" in Mark 5:34*a* in this case actually means "saved." Thus, the word *healed* may be referring to this woman's physical as well as spiritual healing.

It was important to Jesus that the woman who bled for 12 years know and be told with certainty that she was *"freed from her suffering"* (Mark 5:34*b*). She was now healed physically and spiritually. She was saved in both ways. No more shame. No more stained dresses. No more isolation. No more lonely days.

Would you rather be healed physically from a disease or spiritually from the bondage?

Jesus could have merely healed or saved this woman either physically or spiritually. However, Jesus is able to do both. Do we not serve a caring and sensitive God?

Why do you think Christ saved this woman in both ways?

Record the following verses on faith:
Hebrews 11:1

James 2:20–22

What was the key to Christ's healing the woman who bled for 12 years?

She believed with all of her heart that she was going to be healed. She was honest, completely honest in her assessment of Christ. She had heard about Him and had taken it on faith that the edge of His cloak would heal her. As James 2:22 says, her faith and her actions of telling Christ the whole truth worked together to bring her not only physical healing, but also spiritual healing. When we desire to be healed of our shame, we must have faith that we *will* be healed as we earnestly seek the truth in all areas of our lives. What God did for this woman He can do for us today.

WEEK 7 • DAY 5
SATAN'S PLOY OF SHAME

"Satan himself masquerades as an angel of light."
—2 Corinthians 11:14

We first met Satan in the Garden of Eden. There, he tempted Eve to disobey the Lord. Satan disguised himself as a serpent, one of God's creatures. After Adam and Eve disobeyed God, they felt shame (Genesis 3:7). Before the fall of man, Adam and Eve had not felt shame (Genesis 2:25). Thus, one might say Satan did a fantastic job of tricking Adam and Eve to disobey God. So, since the creation of time, shame has reared its ugly head time and time again in the lives of God's children.

Record what Joel 2:25–27 says:

What do these verses mean to you personally?

Look up 2 Corinthians 11:3. What does it say?

Satan has always been a liar. From the beginning of time he has deceived those who would listen to him.

Record your impressions from the following verse on Satan; John 8:44:

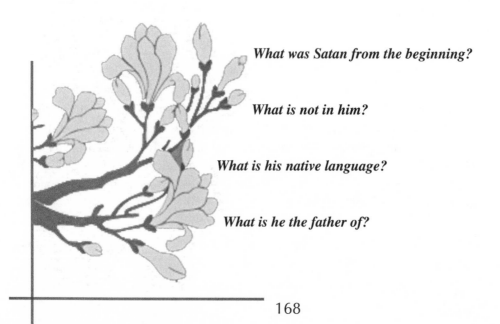

What was Satan from the beginning?

What is not in him?

What is his native language?

What is he the father of?

Now let's look at God. What does Scripture say about God in these verses?

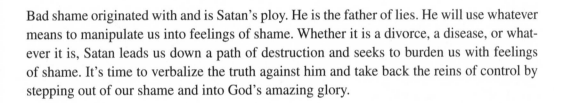

Numbers 23:19

1 Samuel 15:29

Hebrews 6:18

Bad shame originated with and is Satan's ploy. He is the father of lies. He will use whatever means to manipulate us into feelings of shame. Whether it is a divorce, a disease, or whatever it is, Satan leads us down a path of destruction and seeks to burden us with feelings of shame. It's time to verbalize the truth against him and take back the reins of control by stepping out of our shame and into God's amazing glory.

My Prayer

Dear Lord, help us—like the woman who bled for 12 years—to come to you when we need healing. Whether it is a physical condition, an emotional state, or a spiritual attack, help us to come in spite of the shame that surrounds us and to cling to you even if it is only by a fringe. For that is all that is needed. In Jesus's name, Amen.

Your Prayer

WEEK 8

Scorning the Shame Forever

Us

*Therefore, since we are surrounded by such a great cloud of witnesses, let us throw
off everything that hinders, and the sin that so easily entangles, and let us run with
perseverance the race marked out for us. Let us fix our eyes on Jesus, the author
and perfecter of our faith, who for the joy set before him endured the cross, scorning its shame, and sat down at the right hand of the throne of God. Consider him
who endured such opposition from sinful men, so that you will not grow weary and
lose heart.*
—Hebrews 12:1–3

WEEK 8 • DAY 1
THE MARATHON OF LIFE

Hindrances can be everything. Anything. It can be many things. Or, it can only be a few. As
we described in week one, Satan is a very real threat and enemy when it comes to running
our race for Christ and creating hindrances for us. He can hinder us if we let him.

What does Hebrews 12:1a say?

When God says "throw off everything," what comes to your mind?

What hinders you? Please prepare to share courageously with others about how God is working in your life to remove these hindrances:

When you trace any hindrance back to Satan, there is one common denominator virtually every time. Shame. Pure and simple. Every hindrance is a form of shame. Whether that hindrance is short-lived or long-suffered, shame is at the root of the matter. Shame, whether we realize it or not, manifested itself long ago in the Garden of Eden, and we are left to grapple with its hindrances today. Notice that Adam and Eve *"hid from the Lord God"* (Genesis 3:8b).

Are we any different today? Why or why not?

Reflect on Hebrews 12:1a, *"And the sin that so easily entangles."* Sin, as Adam and Eve found out, causes us to hide from God and this gives birth to shame. It is because of our sin that we are so easily tripped up and become slaves to our shame—whether that is expressed in eating disorders, alcoholism, drug abuse, emotional abuse, and the list goes on, as we know.

What do you see as the correlation between sin and shame as indicated in Genesis 3:6–8?

We, in our futile and feeble attempt, seek to cover ourselves as Adam and Eve did.

Record what Genesis 3:7 says:

Do you think Adam and Eve's coverings they made for themselves were adequate? Why or why not?

We must tell God the whole truth and allow God to cover us. It's why Jesus came.

Record your impression of what God says in Genesis 3:21 say?

The only adequate covering for us and our shame is Christ. He is our refuge. We must allow Him into our pain-ridden lives to soothe our souls with His healing balm. We have two choices. One, we can be hindered by Satan. Or two, we can be covered by Christ. Let's let the latter lavish us with His enablement.

Week 8 • Day 2
Persevering in Pain

> *Let us run with perseverance the race marked out for us.*
> —Hebrews 12:1*b*

I trudged wearily on one foot in front of the other. Then another step. And another. My left leg writhed with pain. I was running in my first race, a marathon, and was determined to run the entire distance, no walking at all. My split time at mile 13.1 was 2:20 and everything was going great until mile eighteen when my left leg suddenly stabbed with pain. Now, at mile 25, I sensed the finish line ahead, but was in pure, utter, sheer pain.

Out of nowhere, with less than a mile left to run, my sister suddenly appeared. Spurring me on, running with me, and dispensing encouraging words, my sister became a refuge of strength. Had it not been for her upbeat words, I'm not sure I would have crossed the finish line. However, I did manage to run the entire marathon and felt an overwhelming flood of emotions.

Life is described repeatedly throughout Scripture as a race. Why do you think this is?

What do the following verses on the word race say?

Ecclesiastes 9:11

Acts 20:24

1 Corinthians 9:24–27

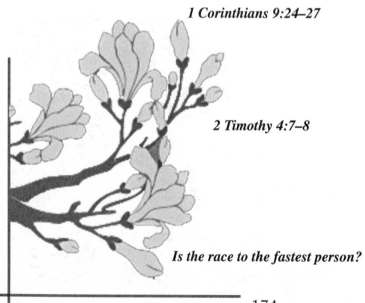

2 Timothy 4:7–8

Is the race to the fastest person?

Does everyone get a time and chance to complete the race?

Does running the race involve training for it?

Will there be a prize after finishing the race?

Before I ran my one and only race, the marathon, I spent many a day training for it. I didn't just wake up one morning and decide to jog 26.2 miles. No, I trained a long and arduous year preparing for the grueling event. I ate nutritious food, I visualized the finish line and I frequently ran between 10–15 miles. So, when the marathon finally arrived, I was as ready as I'd ever be. In Hebrews 12:1*b* it says to *"run with perseverance the race marked out for us."*

Why do we need perseverance in the race of life?

Have you ever felt like giving up? What was your circumstance?

What motivates you now to keep "running the race"?

Life is not a cake walk. We will experience our share of heartache and pain. However, we must remember Paul's words to run the race with perseverance. Christ is our example. He lived some 33 years, suffered greatly. What He went through—even though the Bible describes it—we can never fully comprehend. He pressed on for our sake He experienced unimaginable shame when He didn't have to do so. For our sake He ran the marathon of life. Let's look to Him as our predecessor of how to run that race.

WEEK 8 • DAY 3
THE AUTHOR AND PERFECTER

"Let us fix our eyes on Jesus, the author and perfecter of our faith."
—Hebrews 12:2*a*

I'll be brutally honest. I'm not really a runner. I had a specific goal in mind when I ran—to honor the memory of my friend, Martha. I didn't know what to expect. However, as time went on, I became painfully aware of one thing: I had to finish. Everything would be for nothing if I didn't cross that finish line. What is the key to completing a marathon? Visualizing the finish line.

In your opinion, what is the key to finishing the Christian race?

When I ran the marathon I consistently did one thing: I looked ahead. Never once did I turn and look at the past, or what I had already done. I strained my eyes to look ahead.

Why does the writer tell us in Hebrews 12:2a to "fix our eyes on Jesus"?

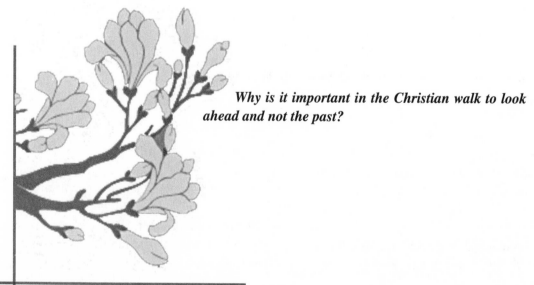

Why is it important in the Christian walk to look ahead and not the past?

176

Has looking back ever gotten you in trouble? Please explain:

Why should we concentrate on Jesus?

What is the difference between glancing at something versus fixing our eyes on something?

We, as believers, need to look to Christ alone as our ultimate source of strength. If we merely cast glances at Him, only sometimes relying on Him, we miss countless opportunities to know Him as "the author and perfecter of our faith" (Hebrews 12:2a).

What does this mean to you?

An author is someone who writes or controls, if you will, a story. Jesus is writing the story or book of our lives. He is in control of the outcome of our lives and faith. Our faith, which has a beginning and end, just like a race, is complete in Christ, who was and is perfect. He is truly the Author and Perfecter of our faith. Are we not then, in good and capable, actually perfect, hands, my friend? I couldn't think of any other hands I'd rather be in.

WEEK 8 • DAY 4
TO SCORN THE SHAME

Who for the joy set before him endured the cross, scorning its shame.
—Hebrews 12:2*b*

We can only imagine the suffering involved when Christ died on the Cross. We do not fully comprehend Scripture when it says he endured the Cross. Death on a cross, in Jesus's time, was a fate endured by only the criminals and the rejects of society. There was immense shame associated with this death sentence. Only the so-called scum of the earth died on a cross.

Having said that, why is it ironic that Christ was sentenced to the Cross?

The soldiers led Jesus away into the palace (that is, the Praetorium) and called together the whole company of soldiers. They put a purple robe on him, then twisted together a crown of thorns and set it on him. And they began to call out to him, "Hail, king of the Jews!" Again and again they struck him on the head with a staff and spit on him. Falling on their knees, they paid homage to him. And when they had mocked him, they took off the purple robe and put his own clothes on him. Then they led him out to crucify him.
—Mark 15:16–20

Mockery. Sarcasm. Disdain. Jesus was not merely shamed on the Cross. He was also shamed in the events leading up to the Cross. First of all, they stripped His clothes off of Him and put a robe on Him. This was the Roman way of sarcasm—making fun of Him by putting the royal color on Him.

When was the last time we were stripped of our clothes, and spit on and made fun of?

How do you think Jesus felt at this point?

Scripture tells us that *"for the joy set before him he endured the cross"* (Hebrews 12:2*b*). That's right, Christ felt joy. How, you might ask, could anyone feel joy in being strapped on a cross to endure incredible suffering and eventual death? I believe that Jesus experienced joy because of you and me. Yes, He fixed His eyes on the finish line.

Just what exactly was His finish line?

Christ's finish line is our redemption. He kept His eyes on bridging the gap between sin and us. Christ was and is our bridge from sin to eternal life. He considered it a joy to endure such suffering on the Cross. It was something no one else could fathom. He scorned the shame of the whole ordeal by taking on shame for our sake.

Look up the following verses on joy and record your impressions of whether you have this joy in your life:

James 1:2

1 Thessalonians 2:19

Philippians 2:2

John 15:11

Now look up Psalm 69:7 on scorn. Record your thoughts on scorn:

Why did Jesus endure scorn?

Do you think Christ can relate to our feelings of shame? Why or why not?

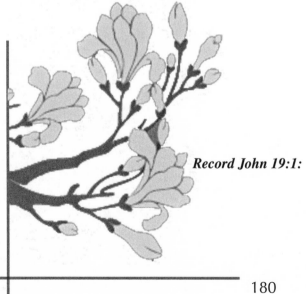

Record John 19:1:

Just what exactly did Christ experience when He was flogged? He was laid bare and His back was open to a lash intertwined with pieces of bone or metal. In case He wanted to flee He couldn't, because He was tied to a post. Many times the victim died here instead of on the cross. The number of blows varied, but 40 was frequently the number victims sentenced to death were to endure.

"See, my servant will act wisely, he will be raised and lifted up and highly exalted. Just as there were many who were appalled at him—his appearance was so disfigured beyond that of any man and his form marred beyond human likeness. so will he sprinkle many nations."
—Isaiah 52:14–15

How badly was Jesus beaten according to Isaiah?

What does Galatians 3:13 say?

Christ took something that was shameful—the Cross—and turned it into something that is full of glory. Our very redemption is rooted in His shame.

However, God took that very shame and transposed it into a love story...His love for us. And His victory! Now, because of the relationship we have with Him, He beckons us to let Him have our shame, all of it, so that He can rewrite our life story. Now, instead of the Cross being a curse, it is a blessing.

Why don't we go to Him, with all honesty, and give Him the shame that hinders us from living a life for Him, and let Him turn it into His glory?

WEEK 8 • DAY 5
THE THRONE OF GOD

And [He] sat down at the right hand of the throne of God. Consider him who endured such opposition from sinful men, so that you will not grow weary and lose heart."
—Hebrews 12:2*b*–3

We have delved into the shameful lives of many biblical women, five of whom are listed in the genealogy of Christ. We've watched as God has graciously and tenderly woven into each of these women's life His healing and has revealed His glory. There are just two people left in God's story of glory. You and me. What do you and I bring to God's table of balm for His healing in our tattered lives? We must allow God to venture into the dark recesses of our minds, souls, and spirits if we are to encounter the Physician healing us. Just as Scripture says, we must not *"grow weary and lose heart"* (Hebrews 12:3*b*).

Why do you think the writer of Hebrews admonishes us to not grow weary and lose heart?

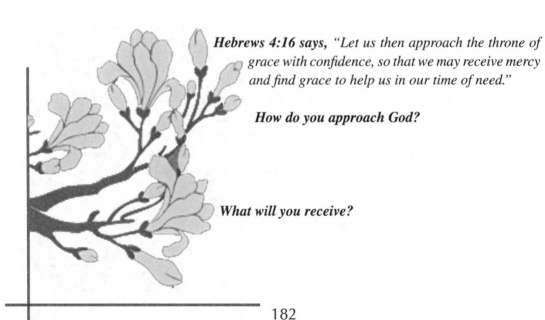

Hebrews 4:16 says, *"Let us then approach the throne of grace with confidence, so that we may receive mercy and find grace to help us in our time of need."*

How do you approach God?

What will you receive?

182

When is the critical time to go to God's throne?

What kind of throne does God have?

Each of the biblical women we looked at was in a *"time of need."* All of us, whether we admit it or not, have critical times in our lives—we need the grace of God daily. Did everyone of the women experience shame? Oh yes. We saw how shame motivated all of these women. Was their shame too much for God? Oh no, not at all. We saw firsthand how God chose to manifest Himself in their lives despite their overwhelming sense of shame. We experienced grace when we saw how God chose five women of shame to be in the genealogy of Christ.

Which woman in the genealogy of Christ do you relate to the most? Why?

What stands out the most in the genealogy of Jesus?

183

Describe the perfect day for yourself and the emotions involved. Why can't this be a reality everyday?

Just like the woman who bled for 12 years told Christ the "whole truth," have you shared your heart with Christ, describing your emotions of shame? Why or why not?

What do you believe is the key in going from a woman of shame to a woman of glory?

I believe it's simple. We merely do as the biblical women did. We give God our honesty, emotions and all, and then wait in expectation, to receive His healing balm. Does this mean we have to be perfect as we wait? Definitely not. The biblical women weren't, so why should we inaccurately think we must be? We are human. We are fallen creatures who make mistakes. Even as believers we sin, according to 1 John 1:9. As we are honest with God, then we are ready to receive His blessings of healing and to see His glory. What God did for these women of the Bible, He will do today for us.

"Christ in you, the hope of glory."
—Psalm 34:5

"Those who look to him are radiant; their faces are never covered with shame."
—Colossians 1:27b

My Prayer

Lord, help me to fix my eyes on You and to remember that I can finish my race, knowing that You will never leave me nor forsake me, knowing that I can release myself to You.

Your Prayer

Shameless

Facilitator's Guide

Thank you for facilitating a group study of *Shameless: An 8-Week Study to Freedom Through God's Redemption*. This study guide includes easy-to-use information, including how to use *Shameless* with your group and how to best address your particular group's needs. The guide allows you to list the names of those who will pray with you for a successful study, and the names of study group participants. You can record thoughts before and during your group study time each week and write reminders for your follow-up with individual participants. Thank you again for your commitment to lead a group through this study.

THE FACILITATOR'S ROLE

Your service involves encouraging participants as they learn on their own, allowing them to share their own thoughts about God's Word on shame and redemption in the group, and sharing your own experiences as this helps to illustrate the teaching in an authentic and spiritually mature manner.

Group sharing can greatly encourage participants to be comforted, not merely by others' testimonies but also by God's eternal truth in their lives. Group members will be asked to closely examine the Scriptures and their lives and then be challenged to make applications. Participants will need your regular encouragement and the example you can provide as a group facilitator. A properly led group and healthy discussion weekly will help each person who participates experience God's healing as well as experience growth.

PRAYER

Pray and enlist others to pray before your study begins. Ask God to help you understand the truths in His Word, to help you facilitate, and to make you sensitive to the needs of the individuals in your group. Pray by name for the individuals who will be in your small group, and for the issues they have asked you and other pray-ers to lift to God.

LEADER HELPS

This study guide provides small-group ideas, plans, notes space, and space to make follow-up plans once your study group completes the eight weeks together.

Each of the 8 chapters includes:

1. Bible passages to read

2. Narrative interspersed with Scripture

3. Reflective questions

4. Prayer journaling opportunity

CAREFUL PREPARATION

Consider what you think are the needs of your group:

- Does your group have counseling support for those individuals who may need to be referred to counseling for more comprehensive, personal support?

- Do the individuals who will participate in your group have strong, trusting relationships with one another?

190

- How many individuals will you include in the group so that the dynamic of the group allows for individual participation? You will want a group where there are individuals who know and trust each other, rather than a setting for this study where everyone is new.

- You may want to ask individuals in advance what particular needs or issues they want to see addressed in the small group setting and how they hope this group will meet their needs.

- Then list or keep in mind the needs and the goals you have for this study. Is your primary goal to:

a. Form a deeper level of relationships?

b. Build up women in scriptural learning on women's issues, experiences?

c. Help counsel a small group of women to reflect on Scripture and the deeper issues of their hearts and souls?

d. Other needs and goals:

STRUCTURING YOUR STUDY

You will need to set aside some time in the first group session to cover:

- Ground rules, including confidentiality concerning whatever is discussed in the group remaining with group members only

- What is acceptable group discussion

- The depth of group discussion your group is prepared to handle on certain issues

- What topics are *not* open for group discussion and how these will be otherwise handled.

- The use of prayer and/or accountability partners

- The organization of your study as a group and individual study helps

- Explain your group study structure based on the input of the group members (study structure can be made flexible; pull out and rearrange the book chapters in the order that works for your group).

- Explain the Bible passages and study chapters are designed for individuals to complete before group discussion. Individuals will find it most effective to write out the answers to the personal reflection questions in each chapter. Many of the questions probe the individual readers' experiences and need to be thought through and distilled before attempting to share with others in a one-on-one or small-group context.

- Discuss in advance what matters group members have stated they are comfortable discussing and what other matters need to be referred outside the group, how, and when.

- Discuss the importance of group members' perseverance in weekly study. You may wish to discuss how some simple incentives might encourage consistent participation.

Proceeding with the Study

How often will your group meet (weekly, biweekly, monthly, in a retreat setting)?

How much time will you have for group discussion?

How much time will your group members commit to prepare before group discussion?

How much time do you want to take for group prayer, small talk, teaching new content, or walking through chapter material?

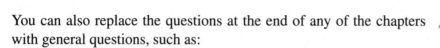

How many weeks do you have to do this study?

Decide which chapters to study and in what order. Fill in a chart with what works best for the group and distribute to participants.

You can also replace the questions at the end of any of the chapters with general questions, such as:

1. What did you read in the chapter that:

    a. encouraged you?

    b. helped you to encourage someone else?

    c. relates to a personal issue you have or are experiencing?

    d. reminds you of something you are now experiencing?

2. How are you going to apply what you studied and discussed?

SUGGESTIONS FOR CONDUCTING THE WEEKLY SESSION

At the end of each session, you will be able to give the group a preview of what they will be studying at home that week. As group leader, you will want to work a week ahead to be prepared for each group session.

INTRODUCTORY SESSION

1. Discuss the following "Ground Rules":

Homework: Each week of the study includes 5 days of personal study. Encourage the participants to complete their home study every week. Their personal time in God's Word will benefit them *and* the group as they share what God is teaching them.

Although it is optimal for participants to complete their homework each week, assure them it is still beneficial to attend the weekly session even if there are weeks they are unable to finish.

Commitment to the group: God has assembled your group. He has brought each individual. He intends to use this nine weeks together to accomplish His purposes in each person and in the whole. Therefore, the group environment should be welcoming, encouraging, and safe. Individuals will share from their hearts only if they feel they can trust those in the group. Please emphasize the importance of confidentiality. Also ask the group members to pray for each other. This can be encouraged in a number of ways.

Perseverance: Life and its demands press forward when people commit to press forward to study God's Word. Prepare your group for the all too real possibility that circumstances may arise that make completing difficult. The enemy will take advantage of anything to discourage them from focusing the light of God's Word on the issues in their lives. He will tempt them to quit when faced with a challenge. Make a written commitment to complete the study, and encourage each participant during the course of the study.

PRAYER GROUP MEMBERS:

STUDY GROUP PARTICIPANTS:

Use this space to record thoughts on how each weekly lesson can be used to minister to participants in your group.

Week One

WEEK TWO

WEEK THREE

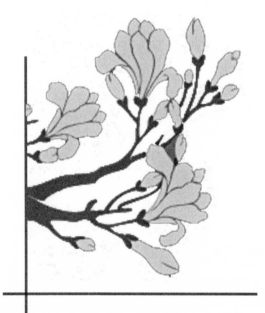

WEEK FOUR

WEEK FIVE

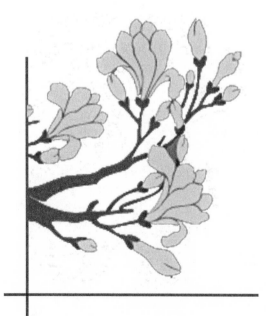

Week Six

Week Seven

Week Eight

STUDY FOLLOW-UP PLANS

Shop to Save Lives

Former prostitutes living in places such as India, Ghana, and Cambodia find a fresh start and hope for a brighter future by making a variety of products for WorldCrafts[SM]. These women become skilled artisans by learning a new trade that helps them become self-sustaining, vital members of their communities.

By purchasing the products they make, you can become a part of helping women around the world find new alternatives to prostitution—and escape human trafficking. Your purchases of handmade WorldCrafts give artisans and their families hope for a better life.

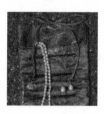

www.WorldCraftsVillage.com
1-800-968-7301 Birmingham, Alabama
WorldCrafts, a Fair Trade Federation member.